A Waldorf Teacher's Notebook

Laura Lavender

A Waldorf Teacher's Notebook

STORBAR & CO

Library of Canada Cataloguing in Publication data is available.

ISBN 978-1-989528-33-4 (Hardcover Edition)

ISBN 978-1-989528-32-7 (Paperback Edition)

First Edition Printing 2024

Front cover image, illustrations, and hand-lettering by Laura Lavender

Book design by Soraya Reis

Published in Canada by Storrar & Co, New Glasgow, NS

For more information contact: publishing@storrar.co

Special discounts are available on quantity purchases by corporations, associations, and others. For details, contact the publisher at the address above.

For more information on the book and author, please visit www.lauralavender.com

These are my raw notes from my full-time teacher training at Ruldof Steiner College, Toronto, Ontario. My expirience at RSCC was one of the most transformative and magical of my Life. I am sharing my notes with the hope that others with an interest in

Waldorf pedagogy might find these records and illustrations interesting, charming, and even useful!

Love ♡

Laura

RSC C

TEACHER.
Training.

_____ / _____ / _____

IMPORTANCE of Handwriting

Writing engages all the senses.

The calendar of the Soul aligns the Soul with the Seasons.

12 SENSES   10 spiritual beings.

Large headed children   Small headed child

↳ Dreamy   ↳ SENSORY

Cold water face wash in morning   Warm Belly rubs at bedtime

INWARD ENGAGEMENT ★★★

★ ★ [ANTHROPOSOPHY] OCT 8/2022

Anthroposophy
does not seek to impart
knowledge,

Balance ○ Playfulness!

The one thing in the world
of value is the active
soul. R.W. Emerson.

_____ / _____ / _____

Grade 1 : Fully guided drawing.

GRADE 2

guided
Drawing
can be finished
later

Don't
explain
punctuation
just show it!

The Fox and
the Stork

▷ Once, the
fox invited

Teacher is continually **STRIVING**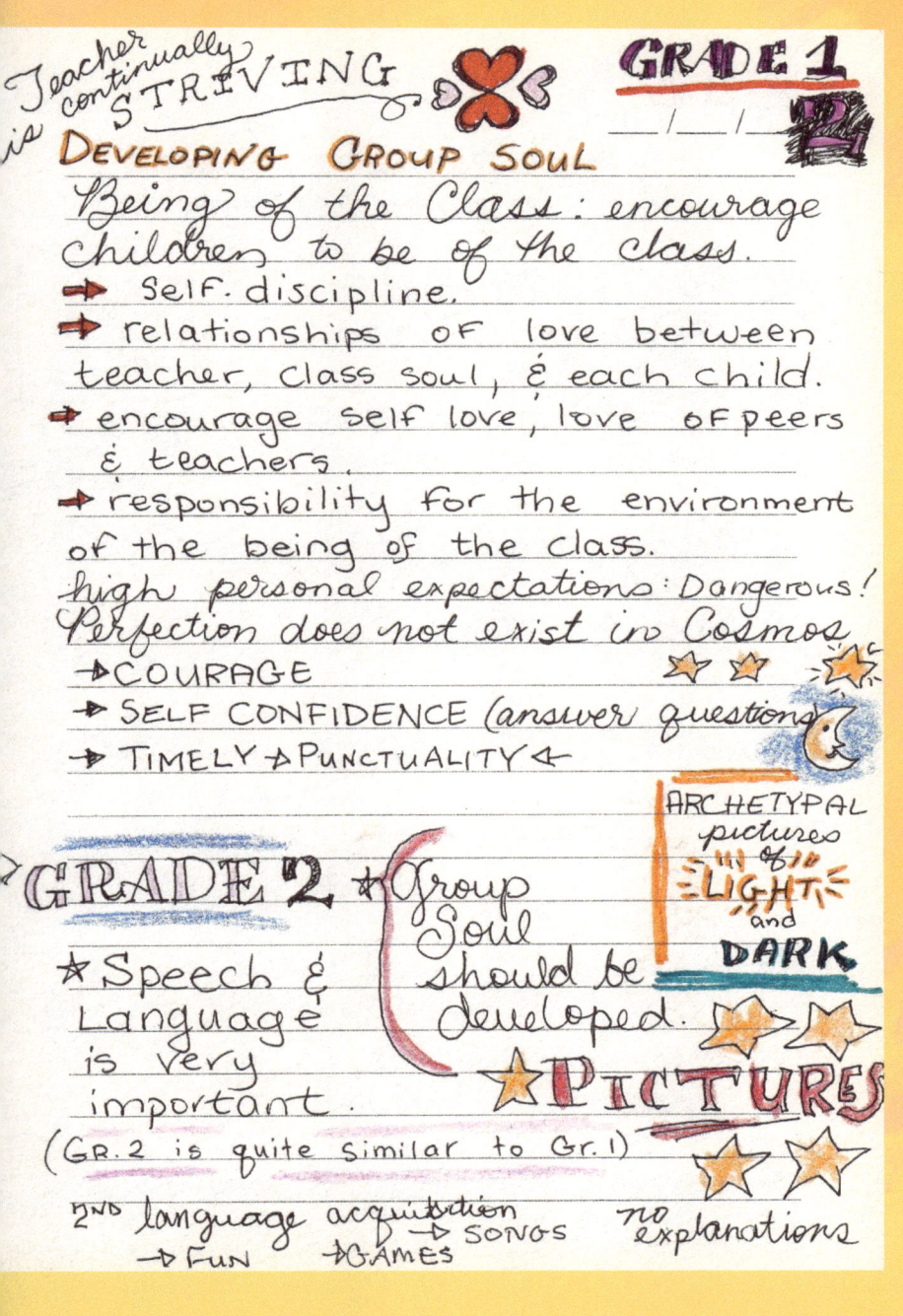

DEVELOPING GROUP SOUL

Being of the Class: encourage children to be of the class.

➡ self-discipline.

➡ relationships of love between teacher, class soul, & each child.

➡ encourage self love, love of peers & teachers.

➡ responsibility for the environment of the being of the class.

high personal expectations: Dangerous!

Perfection does not exist in Cosmos.

➡ COURAGE ⭐ ⭐ ⭐

➡ SELF CONFIDENCE (answer questions)

➡ TIMELY ➡ PUNCTUALITY ⬅

GRADE 2

★ Group Soul should be developed.

★ Speech & Language is very important.

ARCHETYPAL pictures of **LIGHT** and **DARK**

⭐ ⭐

★ **PICTURES**

(GR. 2 is quite similar to Gr. 1)

⭐ ⭐

2ND language acquisition
➡ FUN
➡ SONGS
➡ GAMES

no explanations

GRADE 3

Grade 3 – Three
A Turning Moment

* Old Testament
* Gardening / Farm
* House building
* Punctuation & Speech

CAUSE
&
Effect

▷ DON'T say because.

Adam and Eva walked to the beautiful apple tree.

- Stability
- Go Big
- Earn your Fun

→ Lion, Witch Wardrobe
→ The hairy man
african folk tale

▷ Farming teaches abundance

* Birthday Versos

The Human Being

_ / _ / _

1. Spirit MAN
2. Life Spirit
3. Spirit Self

} SPIRIT

DEEP Study improves spirit

"I"} WISH "Tomorrow is another day."

4. Consciousness Soul
5. Rational Soul
6. Sentient Soul

} SOUL

7. Astral Body
8 Etheric Body
(GROWTH) "ENERGY" (BOUNCE)
9. Physical Body

} BODY

WALDORF is REMEDIAL

Premature Birth, such as puberty at 11, is harmful.

The "I" is born @ 21!
INDEPENDANCE

_____/___/_____

marionette

early
Childhood
puppet

ROD
PUPPET

VEILS
mysteries

etheric
(UNDER)
inner

PUPPETS

Early Childhood Sept. 22

Puppets

★ Storytelling is the ♥ of WALDORF

Components of STORYTELLING

① ★ SPEECH ★
CLEAR, ENUNCIATED
clear speech helps with spelling!

② TELL from the ♥
memorize

③ REPITION

④ no over-dramatization
No squeaky voice. No 'mean' voice.

PUPPET PLAY

TABLE Puppet

pre-academics

★ Soul is ACTIVATED
★ inner Pictures
★ imagination

} THESE SKILLS RESULT IN CREATIVE ADULTS

___/___/___

Grade 1, 2, 3

Be Methodical

Every day the
same thing.

☆ Imaginative content

✦✦✦ Breakdowns ✦✦✦

→ Dividing the class after starting from the whole.

→ Never less than 4 students in GRADE 1,2.

→ If some students do something really well, have them demonstrate.

Corrections

Students are not free to correct one another.

Sit Down with closed eyes.

"I am going to close my eyes and see how queitly you can sit down."

___/___/___

Student can't complete work

    ↳ assign another student helper

    ▷ Check agenda

    ▷ In middle school, ask student

    ▷ Give students multiples (One novel for at home, one novel for at school.)

TRANSITIONS
SONG

"Laurie and Alicia, when we start the song, move the desk to the side."

"Riddle or tongue twisters"

➡️ If children are standing, waiting
- 10 seconds on tip toes
- 10 seconds toes raised
  Count out loud.

⭐ How do you line children up so that the children know the world is beautiful?

- routine
- rythym
- beauty
- safety

_____/_____/_____

plants have + an Ego
an astral
body in
the Spirit
World.

Farming teaches abundance!

BIODYNAMICS /__/__/__

- Holistic, ecological, ethical
- 1924 lectures are the base.
- The farm and garden as a living organism

▷ Endeavor to <u>LISTEN</u> to the land.

▷ SPIRIT + SOIL + COMPOST + PEOPLE

▷ DIVERSITY in animals, plants

▷ BALANCE

| Preparations

		BURY in	
500	manure + cow horn	Autumn (bury)	SOIL
501	QUARTZ + cow horn	Bury in SPRING	Photosynthesis
502	yarrow + deer bladder	SUN for summer / Bury for winter	
503	Chamomile + cow intestine	in earth for winter	
504	nettle Buried for a year	Balance 502/503	
505	OAK BARK / Cow skull / bury for Fall & winter. Balance against disease		

| 506 | DANDELION Cow mesentery | Bury for Winter | Balance silica & potassium |

Working Memory

Facilate WORKING memory

↳ write tasks on the Board

↳ Three tasks at time

| Learning Disability | ADHD __/__/__ |

ADHD is not a learning disability

- Put an ADHD student in the front row.
- Put your hand on their shoulder every so often

⇒ A preview *OF WHAT IS TO COME* can help ▨▨▨▨ remove anxiety

TO BE DIAGNOSED with a ★ ★ ★ ★ ★ ★ ★ ★ ★ ★
Learning Disability, A person must have
Average or
ABOVE AVERAGE INTELLIGENCE.
It means something is in the way
of the persons ability.

Teacher's Process
↳ Ask for help

FOUR LOWER Senses

__/__/__

SENSE of ★TOUCH: tactile

★ LIFE (gratitude)

(SECURITY) ★ Self movement
PROPRIOCEPTION
(FREEDOM)

★ BALANCE

(equinimaty)

3 important capacities
we are building (TIME)

① SPATIAL ORIENTATION

② BODY GEOGRAPHY (SPACE)

(inner awareness)

③ DOMINANCE

Earth Element in Education

↳ Demanding more from children.

→ Children need to know their teacher loves them and needs more from them.

→ Form drawing reinforces life forces.

→ recitations with two other children of same gender.

→ weighted shoes

To HELP Children descend into their BODIES.

Ask more from a child who is hyper / can't pay attention!

___/___/___

Flu Treatment protocol

Zinc 50 mg 1x day @ 7 days
Vitamin C 1000 mg   "
Vit D_3 5000 iud   "
Quercitin 500 mg 2x day @ 7 days

Nasal cleanse (Daily)

Saline w/ Hydrogen Peroxide

50/50 solution

FALL & WINTER PROTOCOLS

VITAMIN D_3 5 drops / day (adults)
vitamin K_2 100 mcg

B_{12} 1000 mcg / day   (adults)
vitamin C

Feeling FLU - Advent?
over-the-counter
     Oscillicoxinum
by. Boiron

From Anthropostical   Infludoron
clinic   by Weleda

COLD PREVENTION, fall through SPRING

Zinc   25 mg / day
vit. C   1000 mg / day
Vit d_3 500 iud / day
Quercitin 500 mg 2 x day.

CENTRE-PULL BALL!

___/___/___

DOWEL

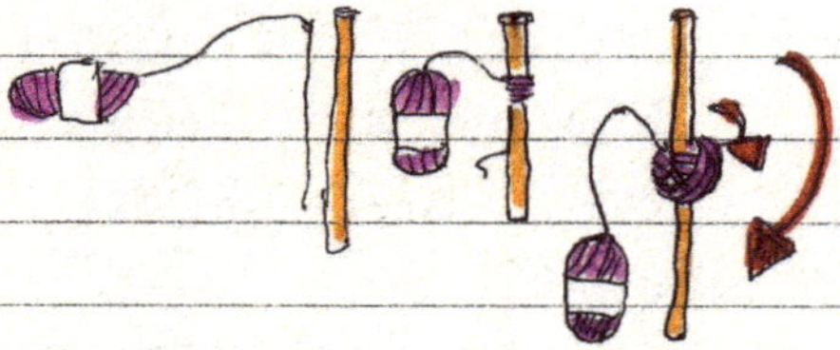

Crochet

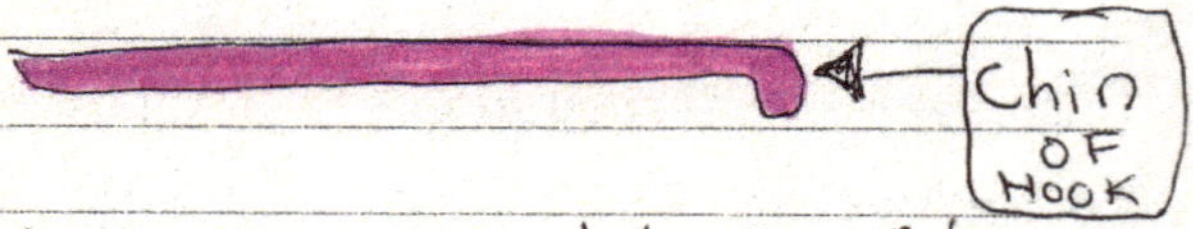

Chin OF HOOK

"Go under the double Bridge
(regular crochet)

Go under the Single Bridge
crochet under 1st loop.

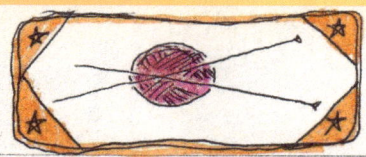

→ Begin with Wool (Cotton is more) DIFFICULT

→ Colours are matched with use of item.

CAST·ON an inch for every stitch

In through the front door
Run around the back
Peek through the window
Off jumps jack.

RECORDER CASE
C/O 22

6
5
2
4
3
3
4
2
5
1

[RIDGES] -6- (START HERE)

To finish 1 eylet row, 1 Knit row, bind off

Eyelet row   K 1
              K 1
              K 2 Tog
              Yarn over (yarn forward)

TYPES of LEARNERS

① VISUAL LEARNER "theatre" Diagrams text/reading

② AUDIOTORY LEARNER

③ Kinesthetic learner
movement
TACTILE

State office hours! | USE Email to Setup in-person meeting! | **PARENTS**

___ / ___ / ___

Meeting with Parents

↳ Ask the parents what drew them to Waldorf.

↳ Have an administrator present. **If Necessary**

➡ Be clear on expectations

➡ **LISTEN**

➡ make notes. Record Keeping

➡ 3 points of action

➡ Send an email summarizing meeting, 3 points. End with, "If I don't hear from you I will assume we are in agreement."

◁ "emails sent end of day FRIDAY will be returned by end of day Monday."

_/_/_ ↙ 3 per year
PARENT MEETING

★ Have meeting start
and end on time

★ Have meeting begin
with parents looking
at children's work

★ Have paper so that parents
can leave a note for
their child

★ CLASS parent can make announcement

★ Have refreshments

★ Have children make an
invitation

★ for 2nd and 3rd meeting
send home some information
to read before meeting

Invest in yourself

NEGATIVE self-talk DEPLETES your piggy bank!

↑ Invest in your own piggy bank with positive self-talk.

↳ I can do it
→ I am **able**
→

PLANTS

___/___/___

GRADE 1

Give each child a plant on the first day of school. All the same.

MATH

$+ - ÷ ×$

~ math ~

Letters are from
[HEAVEN] downard.

First experien
(impression) is
most important

Form #'s the same way ⟹ CAREFUL
PLANNING

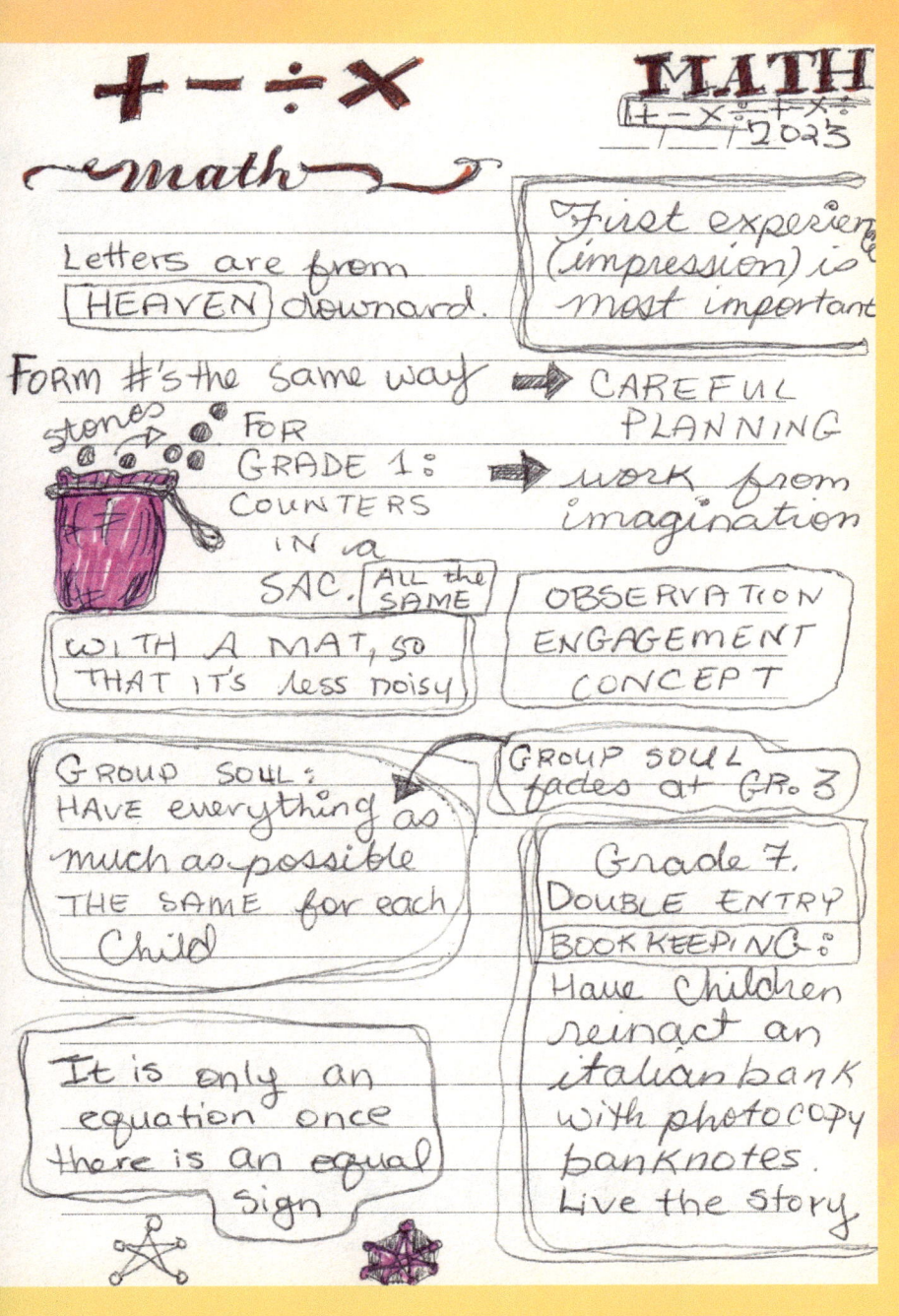

stones ⟶ FOR
GRADE 1: ⟹ work from
COUNTERS imagination
IN a
SAC. [ALL the SAME]

WITH A MAT, so
THAT IT'S less noisy

OBSERVATION
ENGAGEMENT
CONCEPT

GROUP SOUL:
HAVE everything as
much as possible
THE SAME for each
child

GROUP SOUL
fades at GR. 3

Grade 7.
DOUBLE ENTRY
BOOKKEEPING:
Have children
reinact an
italian bank
with photocopy
banknotes.
Live the story

It is only an
equation once
there is an equal
sign

___/___/___ 8 8 ← no snowmen 8's (8) make a lemniscate

How many fish are in the sea?

$$10 - 2 - 5 = 3$$

10 fish, 2 disappear, John takes 5.

Format: ➤ Neat arrangement
- Consistency.
(4.) - SPACE
- MAKE ALL STROKES
→ Consistently.

circle for question number

Address "O" in Grade 2.

THOUSANDS
HUNDREDS
TENS
ONE'S HOUSE

34003

★HOUSES

Top to bottom

give away

⭐
```
  43        − 68
+ 21          52
  64          16
```

WATERFALLS

relationship between numbers

```
 2  1
  343
  6②
  764
  9⑤0
  48②
 31 60
```

I have nothing, can I give away 7? NO! Borrow from the H.

```
    3  6
  3④,⓪⑦,6④
    1, 7 5 8
  3 2, 3 1 8
```
↑ add comma

6 is too small: borrow from the 7.

```
    3  99
  −3④,⓪,⓪3
     1 7 5 8
```

The "ones house" has only 3 and cannot give away 8. Borrow from another house.

÷ ×
DIVISION

Set out ÷
on the left

How many times can
we give away 34?

2 485 - R26

34)84,516 | 2000

−68 000 | 2000 ×34

16 516 | 4

new dividend 13 600 | 400 ×34

2 916

I gave away 2720 −2720 | 80 ×34

196

−170 | 5

㉖

Remainder

21
4)84 ← ones
       ← Tens

2112 - R3
4)845,1

5 goes into 4
once. 1 left
over. 11 goes
into 41 twice,
3 remainder

---

24 485
34)84,516   How many
−68   times can
            34 go into
156 5   84?
−136   BRING DOWN
            the 5
29 1,1
−272   How many
            times can
196 34 go into
170 165?
26

How many
times can
34 be given
away from
84,516

GIVE
AWAY

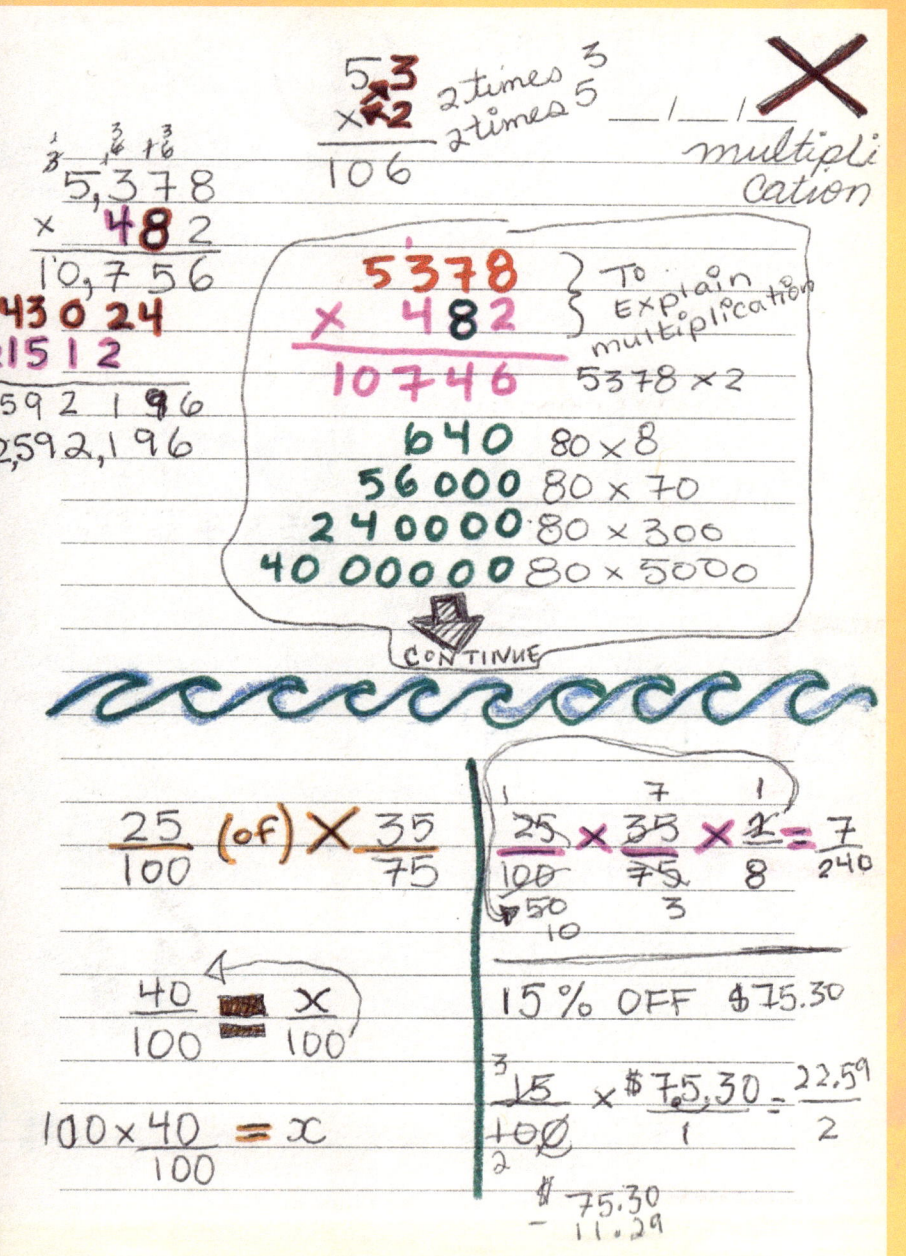

$$\overset{5}{\cancel{5}}\overset{3}{\cancel{3}}$$
$$\times \overset{2}{\cancel{2}} \quad \text{2 times 3}$$
$$\qquad\qquad \text{2 times 5}$$
$$\overline{106}$$

multipli
cation

$$\overset{1}{\underset{8}{}}\overset{3}{\underset{16}{}}\overset{3}{\underset{16}{}}$$
$$5,378$$
$$\times \quad 482$$
$$\overline{10,756}$$
$$43024$$
$$21512$$
$$\overline{2592196}$$
$$2,592,196$$

$$5378$$
$$\times \quad 482$$ } To explain multiplication
$$\overline{10746} \quad 5378 \times 2$$
$$640 \quad 80 \times 8$$
$$56000 \quad 80 \times 70$$
$$240000 \quad 80 \times 300$$
$$4000000 \quad 80 \times 5000$$

CONTINUE

$$\frac{25}{100} \,(of)\, \times\, \frac{35}{75}$$

$$\overset{1}{\frac{25}{100}} \times \overset{7}{\frac{35}{75}} \times \frac{x}{8} = \frac{7}{240}$$
$$\underset{10}{\overset{50}{}} \qquad \underset{3}{}$$

$$\frac{40}{100} = \frac{x}{100}$$

$$\frac{100 \times 40}{100} = x$$

15% OFF $75.30

$$\overset{3}{\underset{2}{\frac{15}{100}}} \times \frac{\$75.30}{1} = \frac{22.59}{2}$$

$$\begin{array}{r} \$75.30 \\ - 11.29 \end{array}$$

FRACTIONS

_____ / _____ / _____

Time is fractions

$$\frac{ABOVE}{BELOW} = \frac{AaSGARD}{MIDGARD} = \frac{Heave}{earth}$$

Numer = member
NOM = le nom

$$\frac{Numerator}{Denominator}$$

$$\frac{(TRUTH)\ actual\ \#}{perfect\ WHOLE} = (FRACTION)$$

← Actually only 1

← perfect

⊖ ⊕

GR. 2 TIME
Fractions!

MUST Start with common denominators

$$\frac{3}{4} - \frac{1}{4} \qquad \frac{5}{10} + \frac{2}{10}$$

Find common denominator

$$\frac{5}{10_{\times 2}} \overset{\times 2}{+} \frac{3}{4_{\times 5}} \overset{\times 5}{=} \frac{10}{20} + \frac{15}{20} = \frac{25}{20}$$

↖ what is done to denominator must be done to numerator

$$1\frac{1}{5}$$
one full pie

$$\frac{3}{4_{\times 5}} \overset{\times 5}{-} \frac{1}{5_{\times 4}}$$

$$\frac{15}{20} - \frac{4}{20} = \frac{11}{20}$$

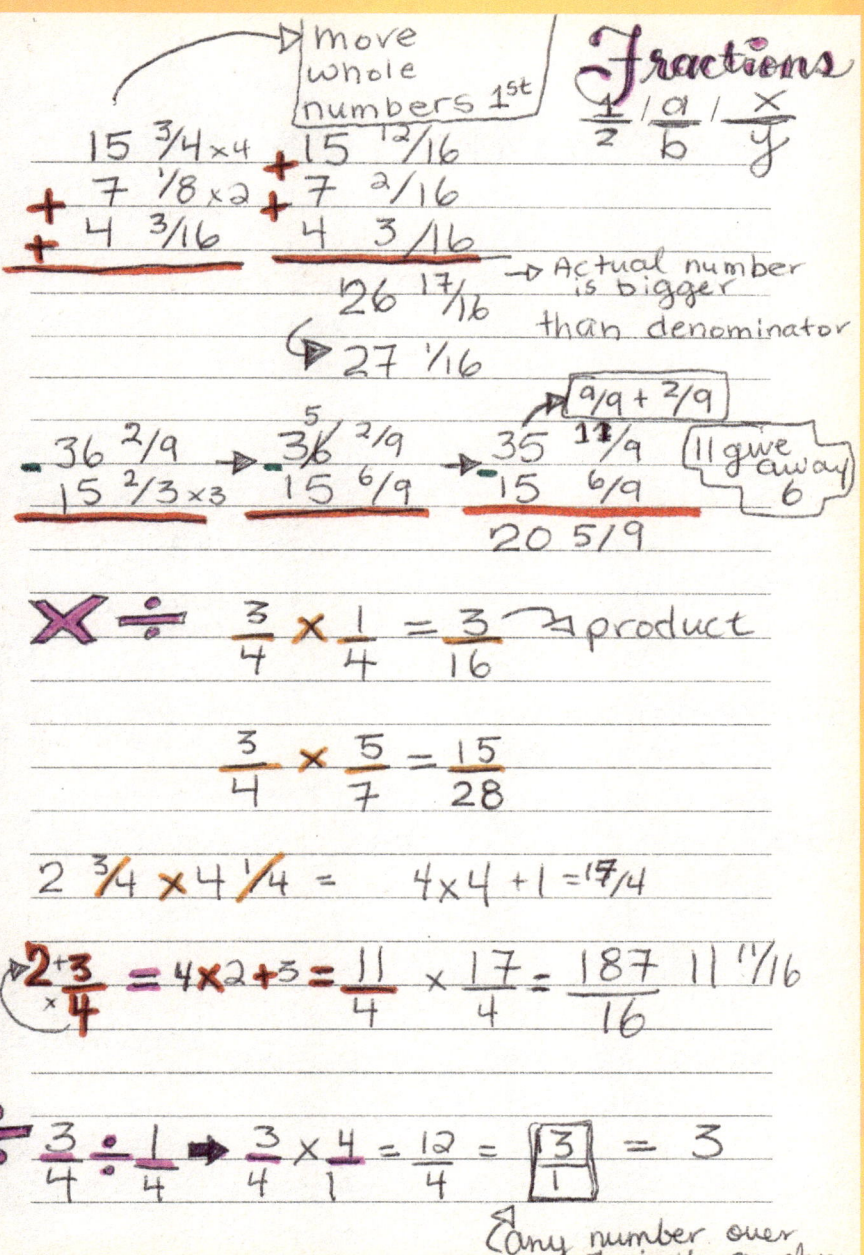

Fractions

$\frac{1}{2} / \frac{a}{b} / \frac{x}{y}$

→ move whole numbers 1st

$15 \ ^3/_4 \times 4$ → $15 \ ^{12}/_{16}$
$+ \ 7 \ ^1/_8 \times 2$ → $+ \ 7 \ ^2/_{16}$
$+ \ 4 \ ^3/_{16}$ → $4 \ ^3/_{16}$
$+$

$26 \ ^{17}/_{16}$ → Actual number is bigger than denominator

→ $27 \ ^1/_{16}$

$36 \ ^2/_9$ → $3\overset{5}{\cancel{6}} \ ^2/_9$ → $35 \ ^{11}/_9$ ← $^9/_9 + ^2/_9$
$- \ 15 \ ^2/_3 \times 3$ → $15 \ ^6/_9$ → $15 \ ^6/_9$ 11 give away 6

$20 \ 5/9$

$\textbf{X} \div$ $\frac{3}{4} \times \frac{1}{4} = \frac{3}{16}$ ← product

$\frac{3}{4} \times \frac{5}{7} = \frac{15}{28}$

$2 \ ^3/_4 \times 4 \ ^1/_4 = \quad 4 \times 4 + 1 = ^{17}/_4$

$2 \overset{+3}{\underset{\times 4}{}} = 4 \times 2 + 3 = \frac{11}{4} \times \frac{17}{4} = \frac{187}{16} \quad 11 \ ^{11}/_{16}$

$\div$ $\frac{3}{4} \div \frac{1}{4}$ → $\frac{3}{4} \times \frac{4}{1} = \frac{12}{4} = \boxed{\frac{3}{1}} = 3$

↳ any number over 1 is the number

Improper Fractions $\frac{\ \ }{\ \ }$ / $\frac{\ \ }{\ \ }$ numerator is bigger than denominator

Do Board-copying work on monday. Write one Sentence at a time.

HEA
We

WEEK __/__/__

control speech

Re-Establish rythym

MONDAY: *Vulnerable

start with *teacher needs to gather.

*RYTHYM *re-establish the rythym
*POETRY *preview changes to schedule
*overview the week.
(not academic)

Don't talk much on monday

Tuesday

adjust yourself to the needs of others
answer questions

Wednesday   Preferably start
ALL THINGS   a new main lesson
IN BALANCE   on a ▓▓▓ WEDNESDAY

Thursday   redo if not our best

Everything to the best of our abilities.

FRIDAY   MEMORY DAY

Bring up an old verse
or song.

SATURDAY

SUNDAY   prepare for week
paint first (practice painting)

_____/_____/_____

Ego presence

___/___/___

→ self work, discipline
→ loving authority

→ Servant Leader

CROSS STITCH

XXXXXXXX

___/___/___

→ grade 4 : crossing. Brings children into themselves

→ aida cloth #8

→ use contrasting colours.
→ start in centre, centre stitch

→ for mirrored projects, use a small mirror so they (the children) can see what the design will be.

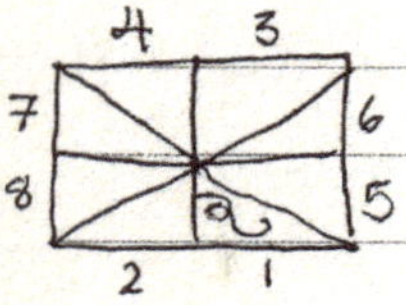

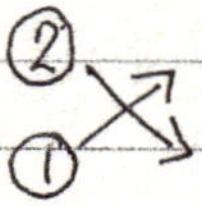

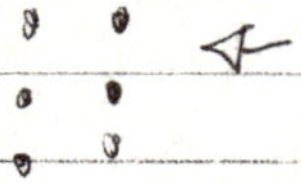

CALLIGRAPHY HANDWRITING

GRADE 4: Pen & Ink.

GRADE 6 : Calligraphy

<u>IDEAS</u>

→ Start With fountain pens

⇨ Use Syringes

____ / ____ / ____

___/___/___

Recititations

* Gestures trigger memory *
movement PRECEDES Speech

This helps memory.

GRADE TWO

* Tongue Twisters: facial
expressions, memory, theatre
skills, articulation

(RIDDLES): have the
students whisper their
answer in the teacher's
ear, to let more children
think of the answer first

DICTATION

___/___/___

HEART - MOUTH - MIND
- HAND - PEN

DR. STeiner
says if we
must assign
homework,
make sure
it is someth
they like!

Poetry

- stay with a poem
for a month

- recite clearly and
beautifully 2-3 times

- after 3 days,
teacher recites less
to deeply listen

FLYING CROOKED

22/09/12

The butterfly, the paper
White

(It's honest idiocy of
   Flight)

Will never, now; it is
   too late,

Master the Art of Flying
   Straight;

Yet has,— who knows so
well as I,

A just sense of How _Not_ to Fly.

It lurches here and here by
   guess,

By God, by Hope and hopeless-
ness

Even the acrobatic swift
Has not this Flying Crooked
      gift.

BY ROBERT GRAVES

★ ★ Biography ★ ★ ★ ★ ★ ★ ★

__/__/__ ★ ★ ★   BIRTH → 10

★ Born in a cold snowy place
at spring. Average
physical constitution: avg,
tall, healthy
★ qualities of soul: creative, sad
interested, shy, quiet
★ positive forces: pers
place of pihit; strength, brave
◯ Challenge: loneliness;

                        10 - 21 years
★ Family values: hard work

The DEVELET
Trigger: fear conflict
                embarrassment
How does it make you
feel? embarassed, shy
  PANIC
  ACT? RUN!! HIDE!!

↳ courage, persistance, resili-
                          ance

PRINCIPLES of DESIGN

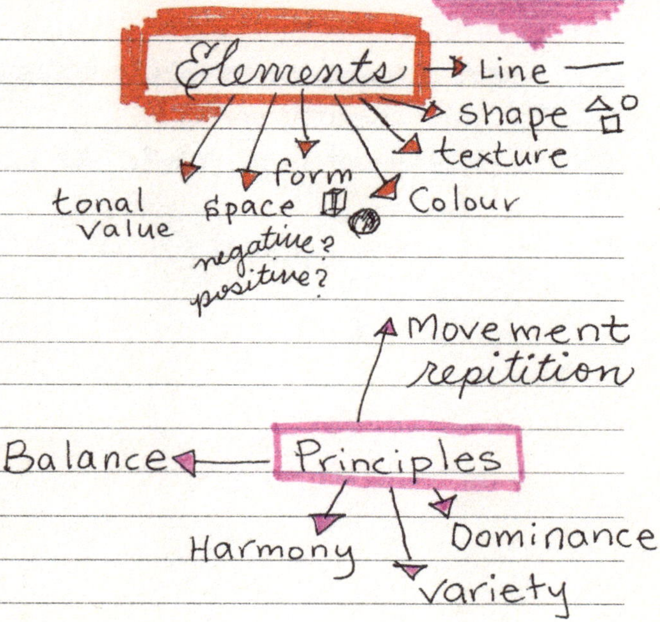

Elements → Line —
→ shape △°
→ texture
→ Colour

tonal value
form
space
negative?
positive?

Movement
repitition

Balance ← **Principles** → Dominance
Harmony
variety

___/___/___

AIR and fire, work my desire
WITH the power of 3x3,
AS I WILL it, so mote it be.

_____ / _____ / _____

MATH

```
  MINUEND
- SUBTRAHEND
  REMAINDER
```

```
  MULTIPLICAND
× MULTIPLIER
  PRODUCT
```

```
        QUOTIENT
DIVISOR) DIVIDEND
```

MATH
+ ÷ - ×

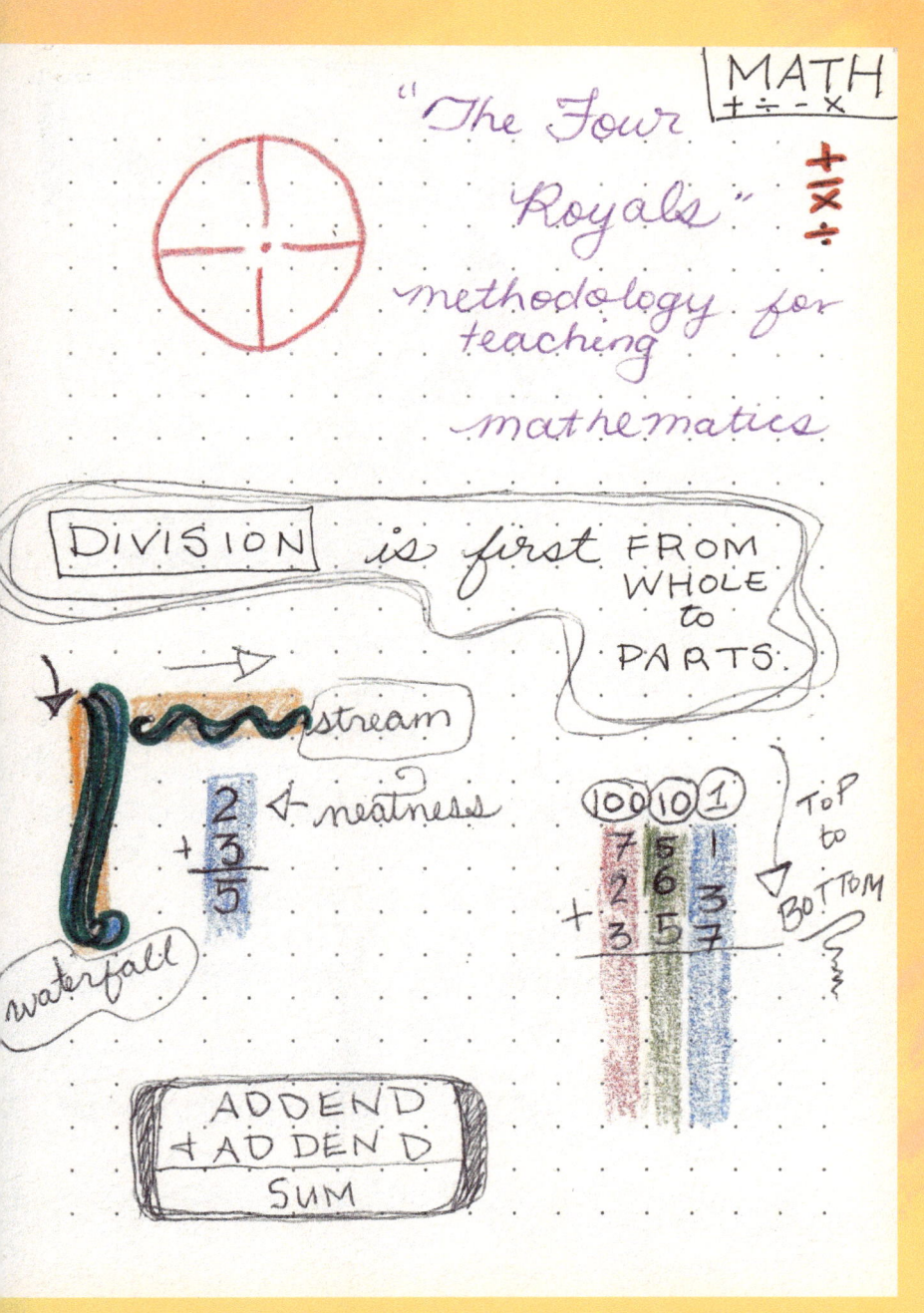

"The Four Royals"

methodology for teaching mathematics

DIVISION is first FROM WHOLE to PARTS.

→ stream

$+\dfrac{2\ \ 3}{5}$ ← neatness

waterfall

⑩⑩	⑩	①	} TOP
7	5	1	to
+ 2	6	3	▽ BOTTOM
3	5	7	

```
ADDEND
+ ADDEND
  SUM
```

PARS PAR TOTO
In the part, the whole

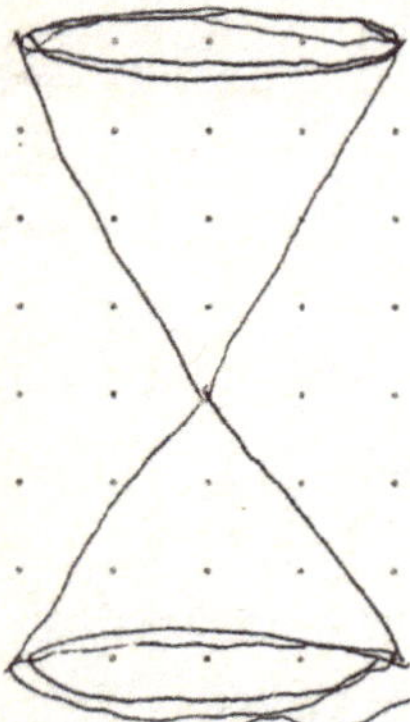

TRUTH
BEAUTY
GOODNESS

girls have strong Etheric

Strong Etheric is
evident in capacity for
reproduction
The cycle puts women
in touch with their health

Men need to pay attention
to etheric, as they are
less tuned in.

Men have more physical.

★WALDORF

Education

HIGH SCHOOL COMPLETES THE CYCLE

Human being is humanized.
Protect Childhood
we can Change. We can influence our environment. We are unique, autonomous, Full of POTENTIAL! We are responsible. We are an individual who has embarked on an earthly path, accepting our limitations & challenges.

★ Receive the child in Reverence ★
MORALITY, ETHICAL INDIVIDUALISM, FREEDOM
To Reach our Potential!

Healing Education

PHYSICAL
SHELL
CRYSTAL
mineral
SENSES
0-7

Etheric: 7
Freed at age 7.
ROUTINE BUILDS FORMATIVE FORCES
Brain BUILDING.
VITALITY · PERSONALITY

ASTRAL
7-14

Ego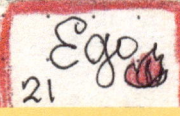
21

Four Fold Human Being

(physical - Annual)

(Etheric - Monthly)

(ASTRAL - WEEKLY)

Ego - DAILY

When umbilical cord is cut,
PHYSICAL BODY is complete
LACK of Rhythym taxes the Etheric

Stories, images, beauty feeds Astral

Ego & Astral leave at night.

PHYSICAL

Earth mineral
GNOMES!

Takes up space.
SENSES

Gnome
Servant of the Etheric

ANNUAL
0-7
2ND DENTATION

Etheric

Under the Sheath of the mother / care giver / teacher

LIFE
Gives life.
FREED at 7

Growth upright juicy WATER
PLANT WORLD

HABIT LIFE PEDANTIC RHYTHM

flow undines
MONTHLY

Astral

ANIMAL
Constantly in flux
Searching for balance

mediates
WEEKLY
Ability to experience pain, joy, sorrow
inner, daytime
at night, it returns to spirit world

WEEKLY FAIRIES SYLPHS
AIR
stories
7 — 14
PUBERTY

Ego

I AM THE CAPTAIN OF THE SHIP.

RESPONSABILITY Holds everything together.

EGO is needed to change habits.

At night, ego returns to spirit. WORLD, WITH ASTRAL BODY.

Angel steps aside

FIRE
Salamanders. Fire Spirits

21

TO BE Human is. a constant state of BECOMING

Precocial / Altricial

UNGULENTS are **precocial**
(hoofed animals)

rodents ARE altricial

{ Human babies } have | altricial |
                        | Digestion |
                        | metabolism |

{ nervous system /
sense of hearing
precocial }

PSYCHOLOGY

SOUL

Ego

Commication
between
inner
&
outer.

soul capacities
Also goes around ➤

EVOLVING

KARMA

WILLING
FEELING
THINKING

HOLDS OUR PERSONALITY
↳ ASTRAL BODY

AGE
21 we can begin to
develope our
SOUL

SPIRIT   Eternal

constantly awakening

Reincarnation
SPIRITUAL SCIENCE

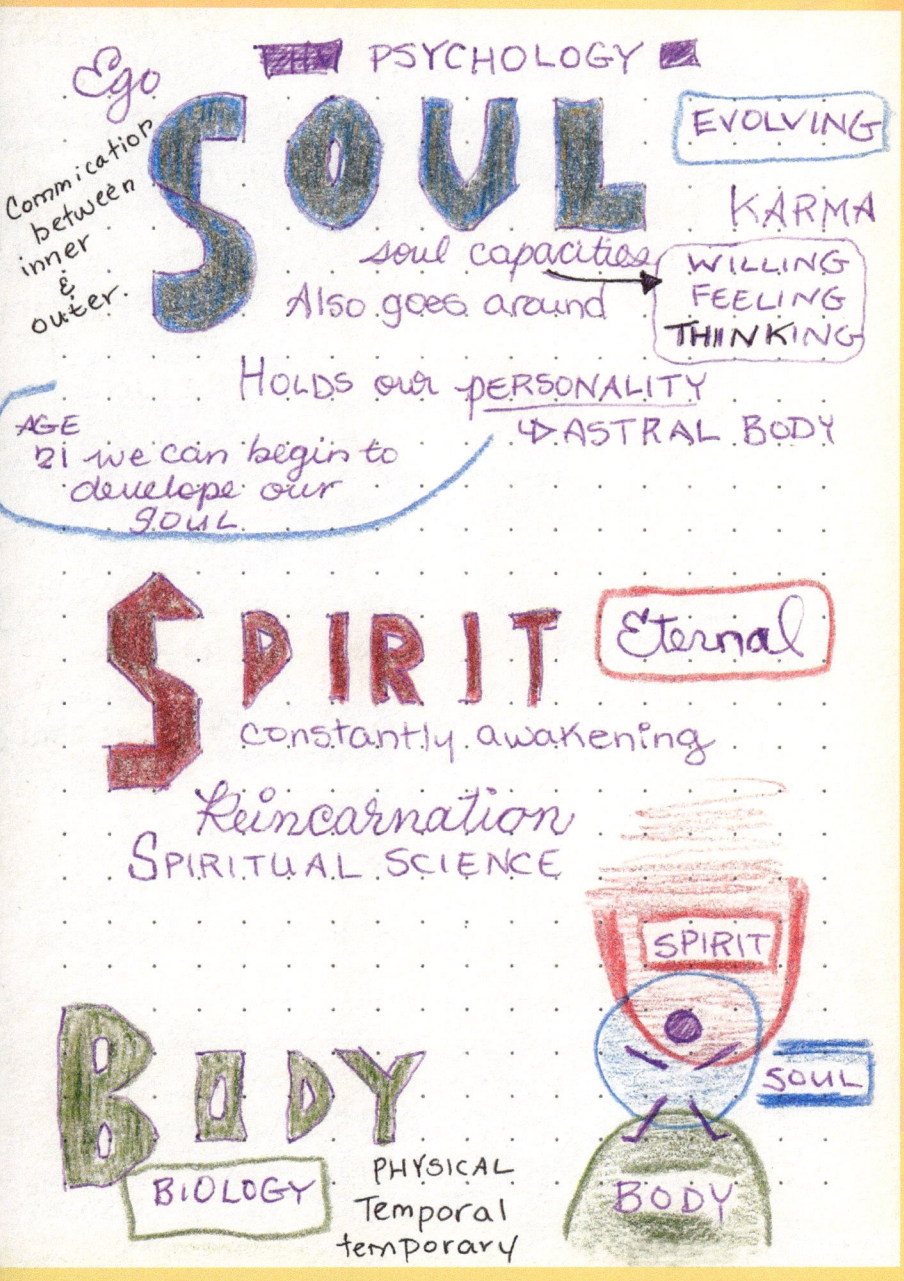

SPIRIT

SOUL

BODY

BIOLOGY

PHYSICAL
Temporal
temporary

BODY

Within the Soul:

HEAD

Active inward
with hard protection

AWAKE

HARD

cool

NERVOUS system

THINKING

AGE 14-21   AGE 7-14

Rhythm
EQUALIZER

FEELING

Rhythmic system

SOUL

mediator   DREAM

HOT

Asleep in our will

WILLING metabolic system

Birth → 7

Limbs

SOFT

How can we support the child's
BODY SOUL SPIRIT ?

CHALLENGES
NUTRITION

COHERENCE
MEANING

OVERCOME
CHALLENGES
WITH LOVE
TRUST SAFETY

→ TABLEAU's of the Day.
→ 6 minutes → set aside judgement

Ruckshau
→ soul developing
→ daily review

Dedicated time to
review your day

BACKWARD
OBJECTIVE
REVIEW

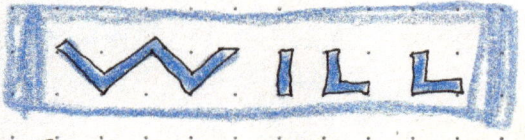

Currently the Will is damaged.
How to activate the will?
Feeling, soul developement
→ RHYTHMIC System.

Spirit is built by overcoming
challenges, and coherence
meaning, in relation to
another Human Being. Then
we become resilient, and
can take a chance. Grow resiliency

michaelmas

4 archangels who
direct the seasons

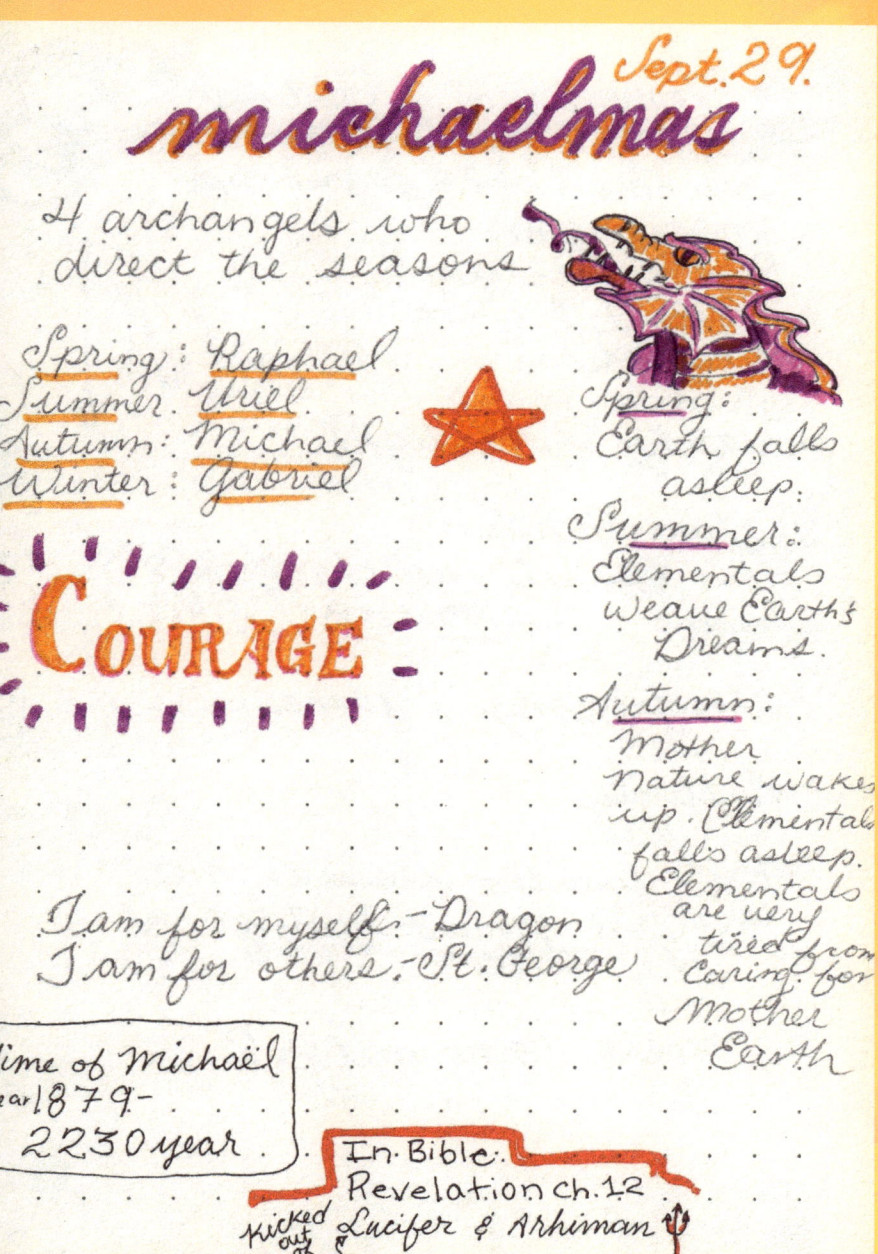

Spring: Raphael
Summer: Uriel
Autumn: Michael
Winter: Gabriel

COURAGE

Spring:
Earth falls
asleep.
Summer:
Elementals
weave Earth's
Dreams.

Autumn:
Mother
Nature wakes
up. Elementals
falls asleep.
Elementals
are very
tired from
caring for
Mother
Earth

I am for myself. - Dragon
I am for others. - St. George

Time of Michael
year 1879 -
2230 year

In Bible.
Revelation ch.12
Kicked out of Lucifer & Arhiman
HEAVEN

Elements of a Festival

- Teachers inner preparation
- Anticipation
- Role of Archangel
- Elemental world
- Symbols

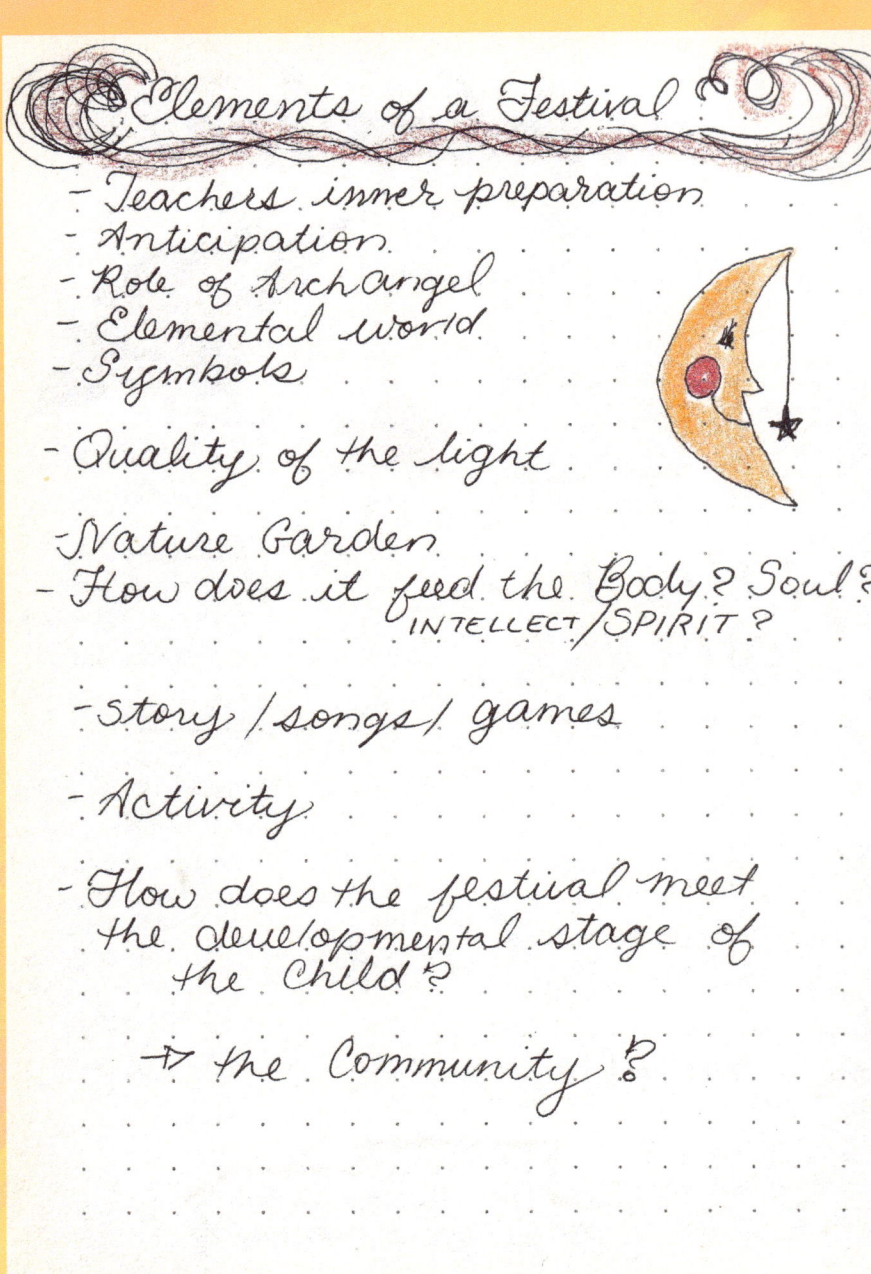

- Quality of the light

- Nature Garden
- How does it feed the Body? Soul? INTELLECT/SPIRIT?

- Story / songs / games

- Activity

- How does the festival meet the developmental stage of the Child?

  ⇨ the Community?

Seasons

Autumn Equinox —HARVEST
Days & nights are equal.

Fire michaelmas Sept 29

Archangel Michael

★Earth Breaths in

→We need to stay awake←

SUMMER SOLSTICE
Archangel →URIEL

★St. John's Day

EARTH ★BREATHING OUT

EXCARNATED DREAM

WINTER SOLSTICE

Archangel GABRIEL

Young Child

- Earth is hard
- Earth Element
- Earth has BREATHED IN

Spring Equinox

★WATER, GROWTH, JUICE
★Earth Breathes out
★Archangel Raphael

★ Create a list of events to do to
★ mark each Season

Birth to ③

BIRTH to 3

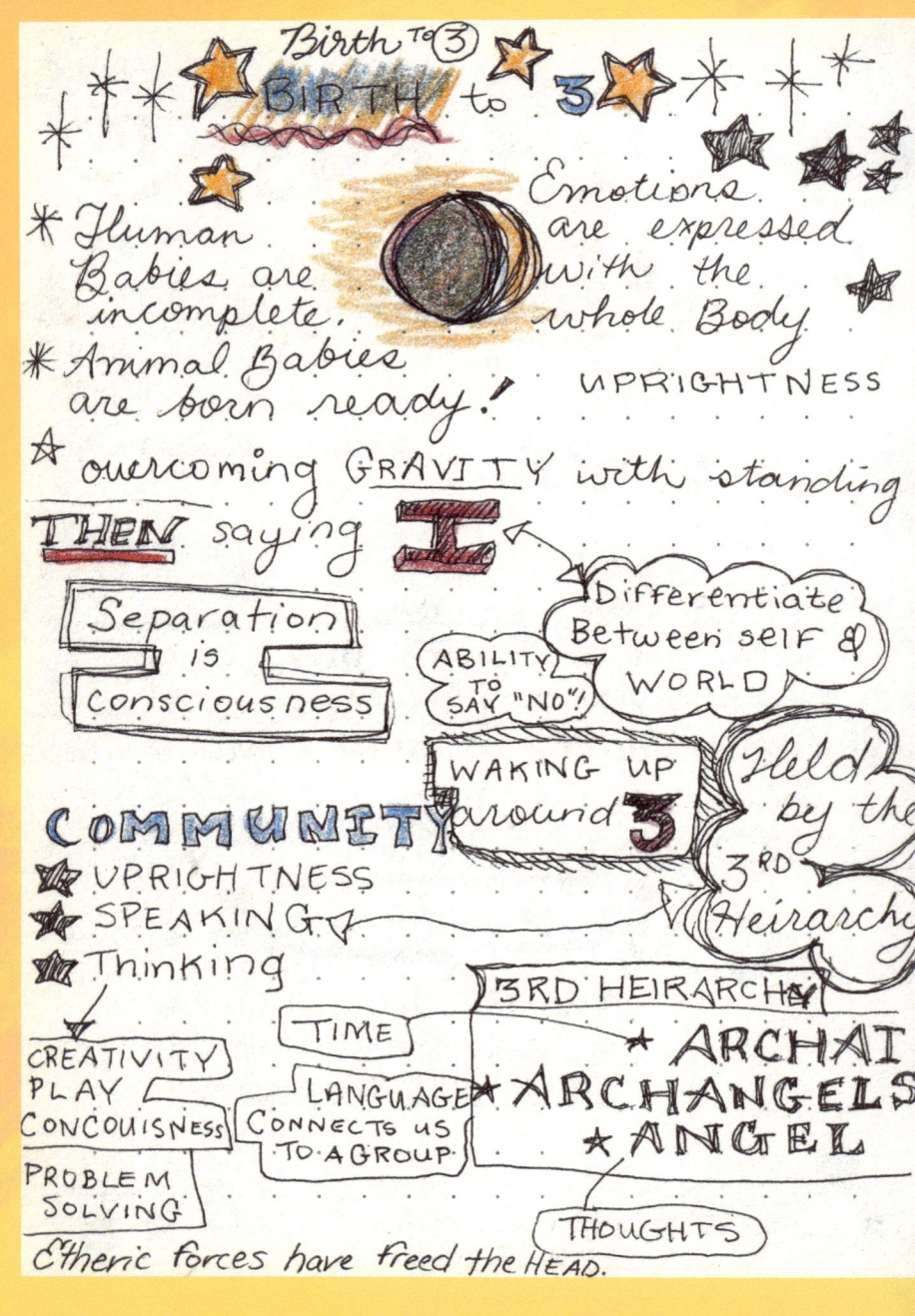

* Human Babies are incomplete.
* Animal Babies are born ready!

Emotions are expressed with the whole Body

UPRIGHTNESS

☆ overcoming GRAVITY with standing

THEN saying I

Differentiate Between self & WORLD

ABILITY TO SAY "NO"!

Separation is Consciousness

WAKING UP around 3

Held by the 3RD Heirarchy

COMMUNITY
⭐ UPRIGHTNESS
⭐ SPEAKING
⭐ Thinking

CREATIVITY
PLAY
CONCOUISNESS
PROBLEM SOLVING

TIME

LANGUAGE Connects us to a group.

3RD HEIRARCHY
* ARCHAI
ARCHANGELS
* ANGEL

THOUGHTS

Etheric forces have freed the HEAD.

3 PILLARS of Waldorf Early Childhood Pedagogy

IMITATION

Devotion } Children are
Sympathy } naturally sympathetic

Physical surrender to the environment
Everything is learned by imitation
model after. Travel with each other.
Breathing into what the other Breathes
MOVEMENT is attractive, & imprints
Deeply into the Childs Body organization.
(Physical, ETHERIC, Astral organization)
Moral significance: child can
sense vibrations.
Around 7, imitation looses appeal
and LOVING AUTHORITY

LANGUAGE

Learn through { Pre-Academics
PLAY is how children
make sense of
Protect Play the world.

Fire
Fairies to
come
us

Rhythm is Breathing

RHYTHM

FLOW

Rhythm is life giving

Predictable.

3 years

5 years

children grow up

& THEN

← OUT →

a moment of consciousness:

Reverance

attention TO DETAILS

GRATITUDE

protects the Vulnerability

Spirit

physical

GRATITUDE

WHY?

Playful conversation

engagement

3 → 5 years

★ ANNOUNCEMENT of **I**

★ CAN PLAY with other children

★ JOY and

★ can do for themselves

★ Angel is still there. BUT THEY are more of THE WORLD

★ Language is expanding

Reverance is attention to details

" **I** "

Differentiate between Self & WORLD

no!

Be worthy of Imitation

Imagination ↔ Imitation
(Daily events)

5 6 7 years

neck!
teeth!

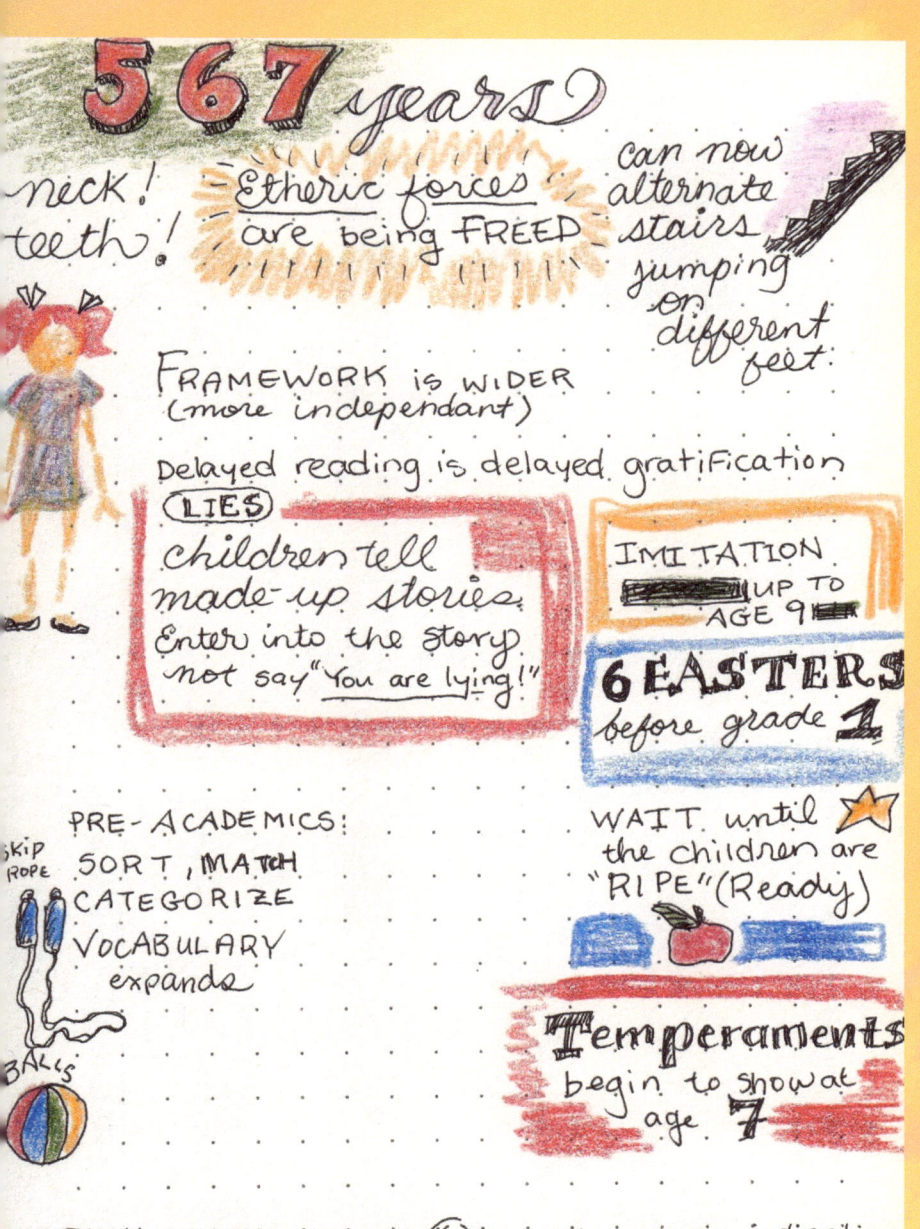

Etheric forces are being FREED

can now alternate stairs jumping on different feet.

FRAMEWORK is WIDER (more independant)

Delayed reading is delayed gratification

(LIES)
children tell made-up stories.
Enter into the story
not say "You are lying!"

IMITATION UP TO AGE 9

6 EASTERS before grade 1

PRE-ACADEMICS:
SORT, MATCH
CATEGORIZE
VOCABULARY expands

SKIP ROPE

BALLS

WAIT until the children are "RIPE" (Ready)

Temperaments begin to show at age 7

CHILDS Demeanor at (6) can give up an indication of the childs adolescence.

Re-aquanting Children with human life on Earth

Teach about #7:
Tell story of Snow
white at end of lesson
Tuesday. Wednesday,
remind class prior
to new
Lesson

etheric Body
is the Body
of Memory

CLASSROOM MANAGEMENT
overview of main lesson.

A STRUCTURE

BEFORE School

Attendance

R.S. STUDENTS CAN BE PAIRED TO DO ATTENDANCE.

8:30-8:45 GREETING

MORNING VERSE Begins lessons

MORNING Verse

OPENING EXERCISES: reincarnate after the night

30 MINUTES — 15 min. might work

WEEKENDS ARE EXCARNATING, TOO

When are they in?

Review OF YESTERDAYS NEW TEACHING.

1. ACTIVATE WILL & MEMORY (Etheric)
2. ACTIVATE FEELING (astral)
3. TEASE THE THINKING (ego)

New Teaching create a "carriage of imagination"

★ clear instruction
★ TIGHTLY PLANNED.

WORK TIME
★ 15-20 minutes (GRADE 1)
★ 45-60 minutes (Grade 8)

STORY CAN BE CRITICAL

AT GRADE 4, Some students can read the Day's schedule.

catching up:

If a child is absent:

ask two children to

retell story over recess

which is an → INBREATH
Brain GAME,
stretching.

Attendance:
create an activity to keep
children busy while attendance
is delivered.

Singing is an outbreath.

Choose don't Ask! → May
                    → PLEASE

"kayla, please put
the date on the
board in your
nicest cursive handwriting."

CAN COULD

Focus
Balance on one Foot

GRADE 1 →

Everything
CROSSING
in the physical
BODY builds focus.

PERSONAL SPACE

Distance of one handshake

Add a Jewel to Sword

on Black Board

for good behavior.

Learning
a new song
is a inbreath

Singing is an outbreath.

Recitation is an inbreath

MARCHING is an out breath.

Alternate these to support Breathing

STANDING & SITTING

STAND and SING to wake up class Before new teachings

Storytime :- Leave title until the end.
              - use gestures

Use GLOCKENSPIEL TO call
children to sit down in morning

CLASSROOM
GROUP SOUL

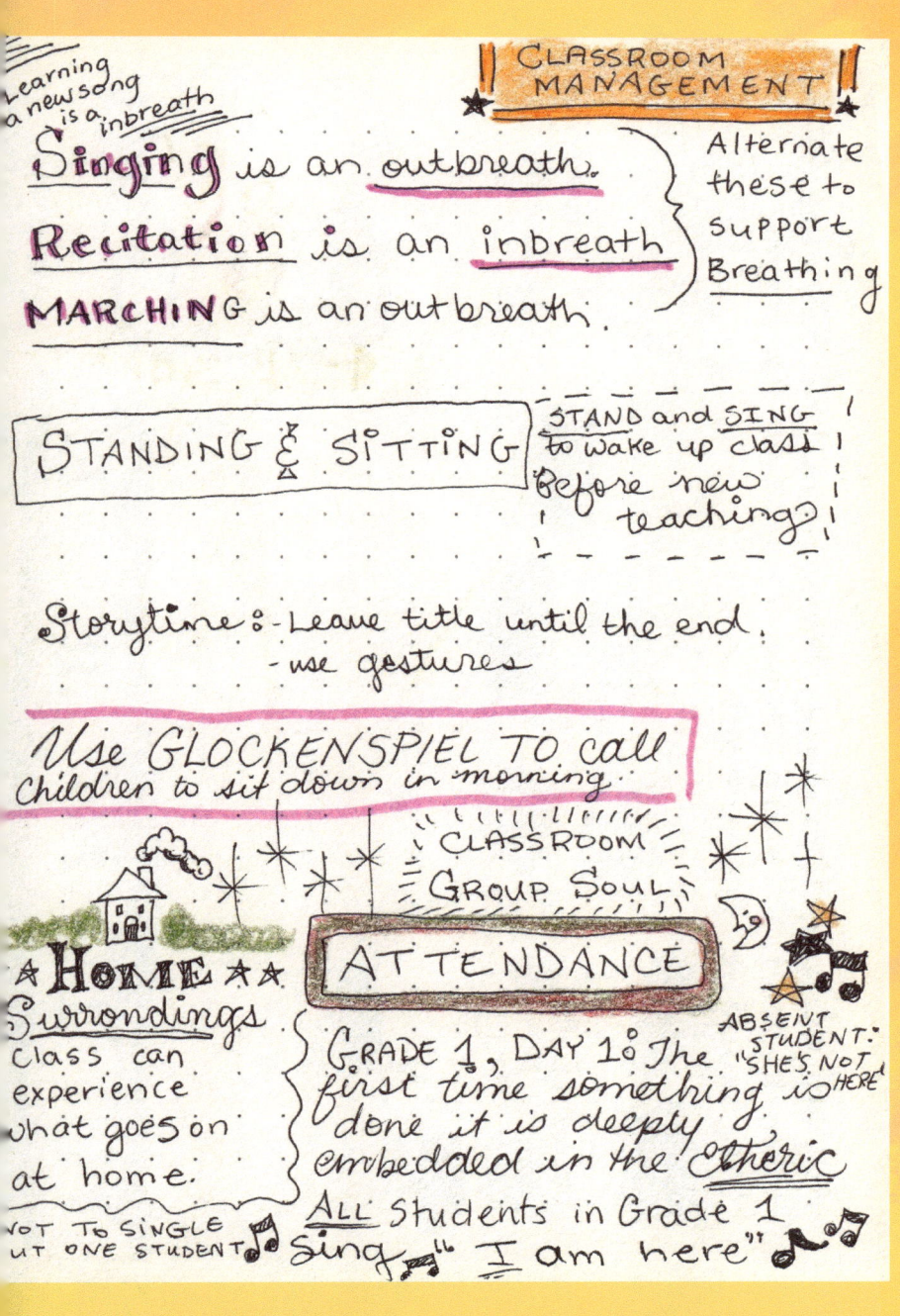

A HOME
Surroundings
class can experience what goes on at home.

ATTENDANCE

GRADE 1, DAY 1° The first time something is done it is deeply embedded in the Etheric

ABSENT STUDENT:
"SHE'S NOT HERE"

NOT TO SINGLE OUT ONE STUDENT

ALL Students in Grade 1 Sing " I am here"

Ask children to distribute items from left to right, from behind. Pick up items from left to right. One student from each row.

THREE DAY RHYTHM

New: Day 1 lesson

review: Day 2

work: Day 3 time

Review: 3 questions

1. FACTUAL
2. ASTRAL (feeling)
3. EGO question

⭐ 3 DAY RHYTHM

M T W T F

Review / New teaching / ≡WORK≡

Review / New teaching: A / ≡WORK≡

Review / New / Work

≡Review≡ / A / New / ≡WORK TIME≡ / A

NEW / REVIEW

You don't ask what the moral of the story is.

Two nights. Sleeping over the new teaching.

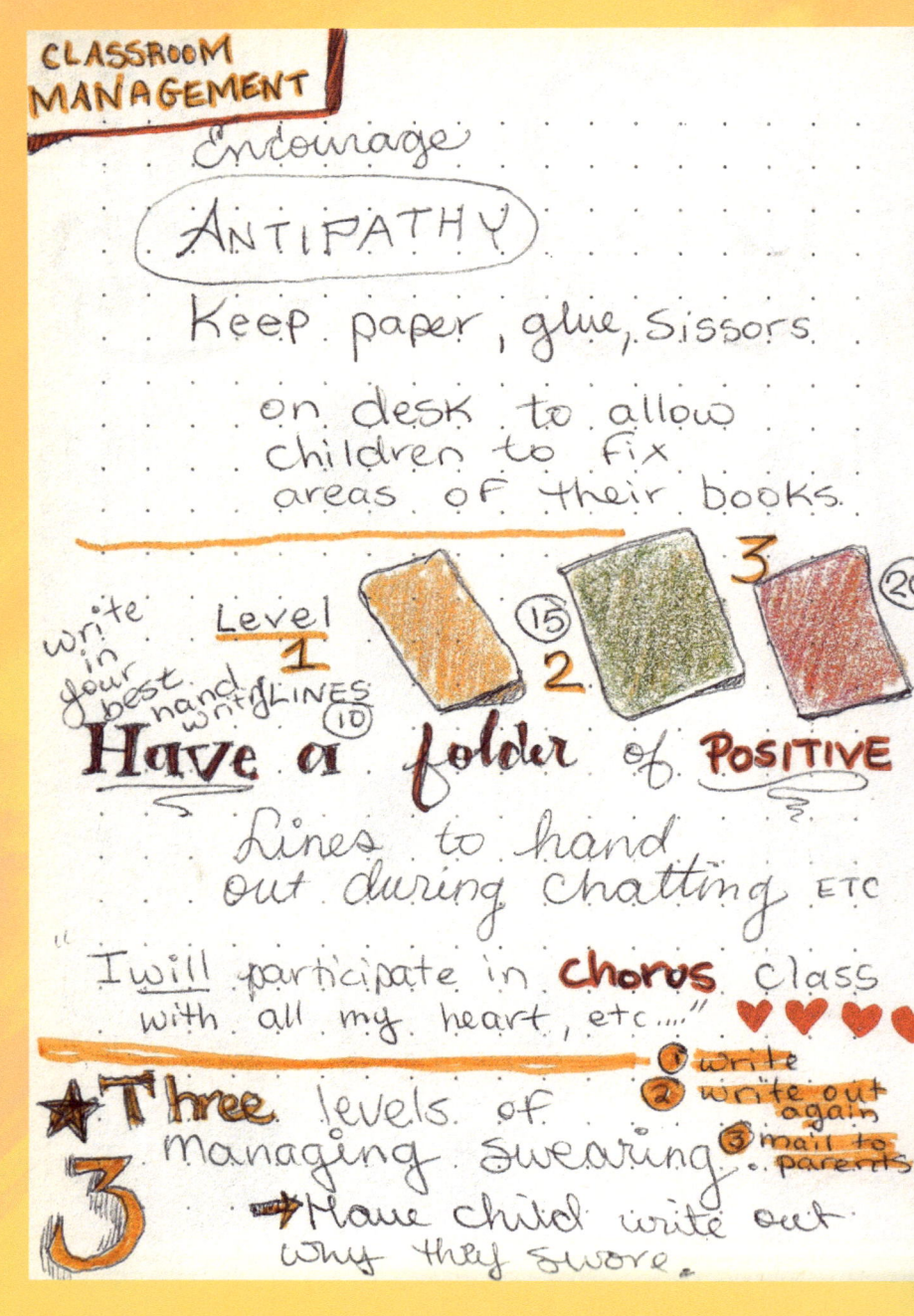

CLASSROOM MANAGEMENT

Entourage

ANTIPATHY

Keep paper, glue, scissors

on desk to allow
children to fix
areas of their books.

write in your best hand writing

Level 1 LINES 10

15

2

3

20

Have a folder of POSITIVE

Lines to hand
out during chatting ETC

"I will participate in **chorus** class
with all my heart, etc...." ♥ ♥ ♥ ♥

★ Three levels of
managing swearing

3

① write
② write out again
③ mail to parents!

↱ Have child write out
why they swore.

WHOLE CLASS misbehaving

More than 4 Children MisBEHAVING

CONSEQUENCES (fitting) to the PROBLEM

"All staying behind at recess. Row 1, go get a book with pictures & look at the picture for 3 minutes. Then, close the book, and raise your hand and describe the picture."

Teach classroom and school culture.
→ raise hand to speak
→ Quiet chatting during social times
→ Noisyness outside!

Factual Question

"A STORY IS A PICTURE.

Starting with the word ___, recreate the story"

Feeling Question

" How did you feel when... "
" How did ||character x|| feel... "

OCCASSIONALY Recreate the whole story in the review To nurture speaking skills, and pull up pieces of the story from the Etheric

Ego Question

" If you were the author of the story, how would you change the ending... "
" what other ▭ could have been in ▭ ... "

Grade 4

In waldorf, children experience the 9 year change in Grade 4.

9 year old Change.

{ Insecurity.
Bloody-minded,
Earthy nature
"It's not fair."

→ STORIES

→ Stories about terrifying creatures Sneaky characters. Giants. DARKNESS

The war of the All against the All.

Shyness: an inner insecurity

Shyness with Performance: HAND Puppets!

Get child to use PUPPETS.

Kindergarden children learn through...

nerve & sense process

Early child teacher needs to study the nervous system

gesture

Class teacher: work of heart and lung

gesture

imagination

Ask what do you think

Don't JUDGE

mental images

Learning in EC - Imitation
L.S. - Emulation
H.St - transformation / understanding

↙ Loving Authority

Stand on your desk and recite poetry!

EARLY PUBERTY
melatin from PINEAL GLAND helps us sleep, and delays puberty. Too much light causes Pineal glant to not secrete as much melatin.

augere → latin word for "swell"

authority

Cause your students to become bigger than themselves.

Adolescents learn through Processes of metabolism

by making it their own

ADOLESCENCE

gesture

INVOLUTION

TRANSFORMATION

teaching from 'I'

10th → 11th GRADE

Umstülpen
Umstülpung

HIGH SCHOOL teacher must be AN AUTHENTIC PERSON

ALCHEMIZING
DISCOVERING
UNDERSTANDING
Deconstructing
transforming

HIGH SCHOOL STUDENTS ARE the world.
akin to the metabolic process.

Choice

make it your own

GR. 9 : review on board

GR. 10 review w linking

WILL

teacher

subject

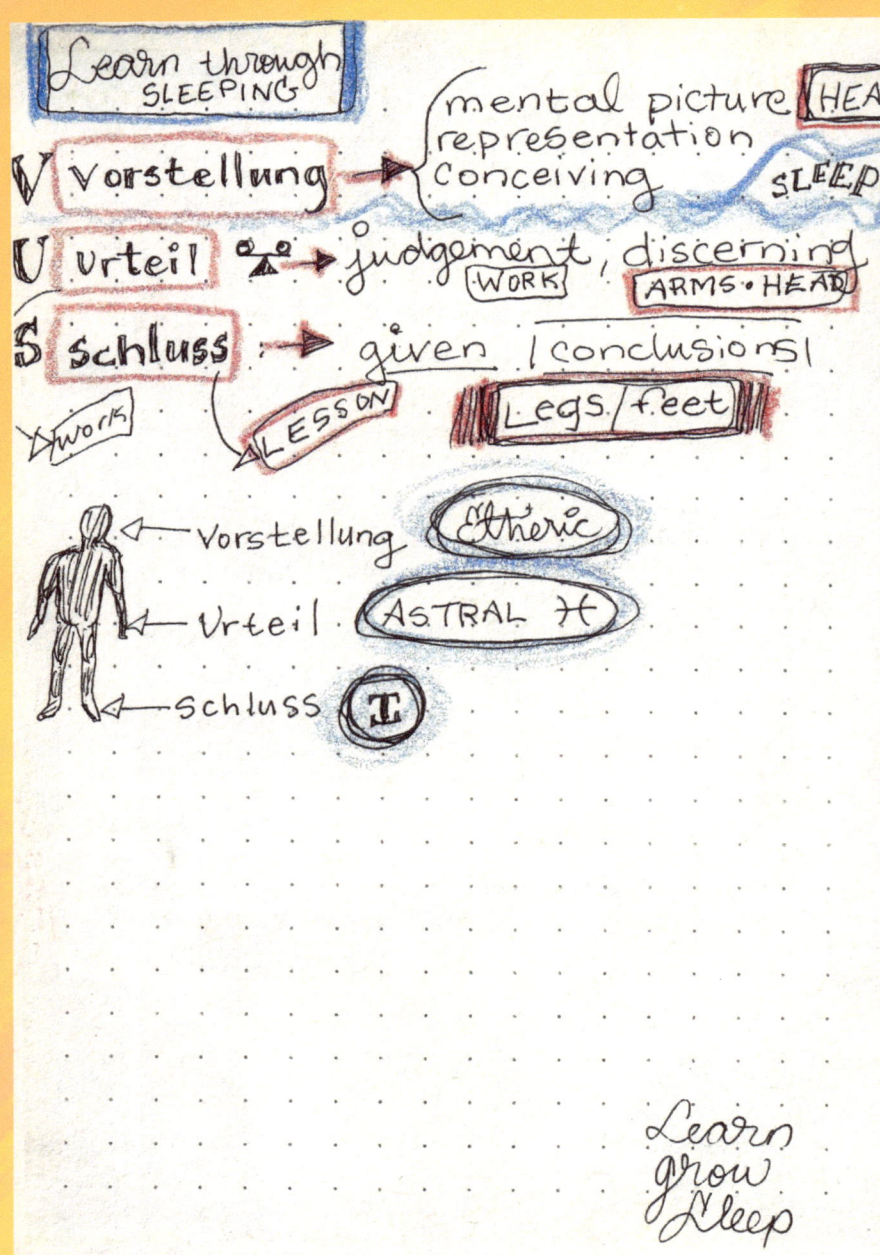

Learn through SLEEPING

V **Vorstellung** → mental picture representation conceiving [HEAD] SLEEP

U **Urteil** → judgement [WORK], discerning [ARMS·HEAD]

S **schluss** → given |conclusions| Legs/feet

[work] [LESSON]

Vorstellung ← Etheric

Urteil ← ASTRAL ♓

schluss ← I

Learn grow Sleep

HIGH SCHOOL CURRICULUM

ADOLESCENCE

GRADE — BODY — GESTURE — THINKING — GUIDING QUESTION

BOOK of NATURE + CULTURE

WHAT?

9
- Physical expansion

mineral History OBSERVING

10
- Etheric organism

PHYSICS ACIDS BASES
Mecanics titration
(Balance)
EQUILIBRIUM Humanities essays'
BALANCE
SCALES

Comparitive HOW?
Process

LANGUAGE

Physical

metaphysical → beyond the physical senses

11 grade
ASTRAL
INVISIBLE GESTURE

#MUSIC #BOTANY #[ATOMIC THEORY]
Quest, Journey
(but not for something)

Why?

"Ana Lusein?"
Analysis

I

ARCHITECTURE
LIGHT. OPTICS
BIOLOGY. ZOOLOGY

HISTORY→SYMPTOMATICALLY
Novels

Tower with a spiral staircase

High School
no home room
* Waldorf is behind

WHO ⊙

CURRICULUM

kindergarten: home : sheath
lower school : school : sheath
High School : community : sheath

Hülle sheath

12

Rückshau

Perhaps divide
the children
into groups,
one group each
night of the
week

How we
see them

Image
Understanding
How we help.

Image
↓   ↓
time   Space — sleep
       health ~ food

Learn
drawing
handwork

Do less
but
Do it well

GR.I observations
- Handshake?
- Hand writing?

— Christoff
recommends 1
week Observation

Self
Discipline

No family
information

No medical
diagnosis

Objective
rather than
Subjective

No family
involvement

Plan & Prepare

Weekly observation
↳ 5 children PATT
per day.
→ Keep in locked
binder.
→ Rotate children
from ~~week~~ to week,

CHILD STUDY — OBSERVATION

* Free ourselves from bias, preferences

* allow the subject to reveal themselves.

OBSERVATION:
→ Discipline, practice, training.

white magic

inner
work
tunes
our
instrument

4 FOLD
→ physical
being
→ Life
energy
→ soul
→ self
identity

Listen

BE Curious

Look CLOSELY

Absorb everything

CLASS STUDY
↳ GR. 1
GR. 5 (9 yr. change)

2 FOLD. HUMAN BEING.

IS
RNS

3 fold human

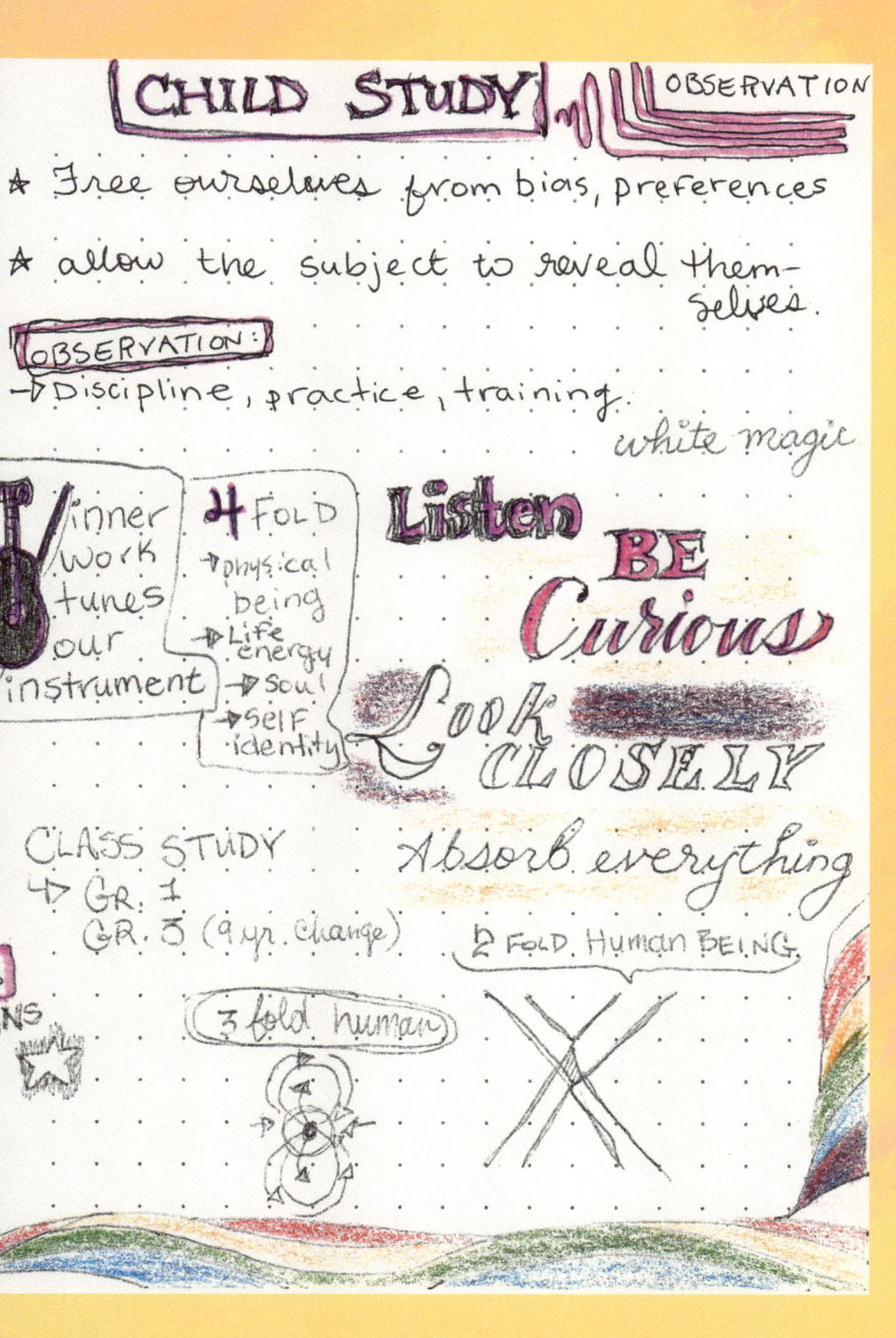

Help Children find

BALANCE

through observation

MOVEMENT

Movement improves cognitive
abilities

use a
MAP for
the inside
of desk

Yasmein's Non-negotiables

- **Handshake** — morning & afternoon
- ⭐ **Verses** morning
- ⭐ Invite the Angels
- ⭐ Clear the Clutter
- A Welcoming Warm Space
  - Friday organize desks

yasmeen_mamdami@hotmail.com

SLEEP

BALANCE ⭐

We have the will to work

that into this our work

                    may flow,

that which, from out the
spiritual world

Working in soul and spirit

In ~~life~~ life and body
(in soul and spirit)

strives to become human
    within us.

    R.S

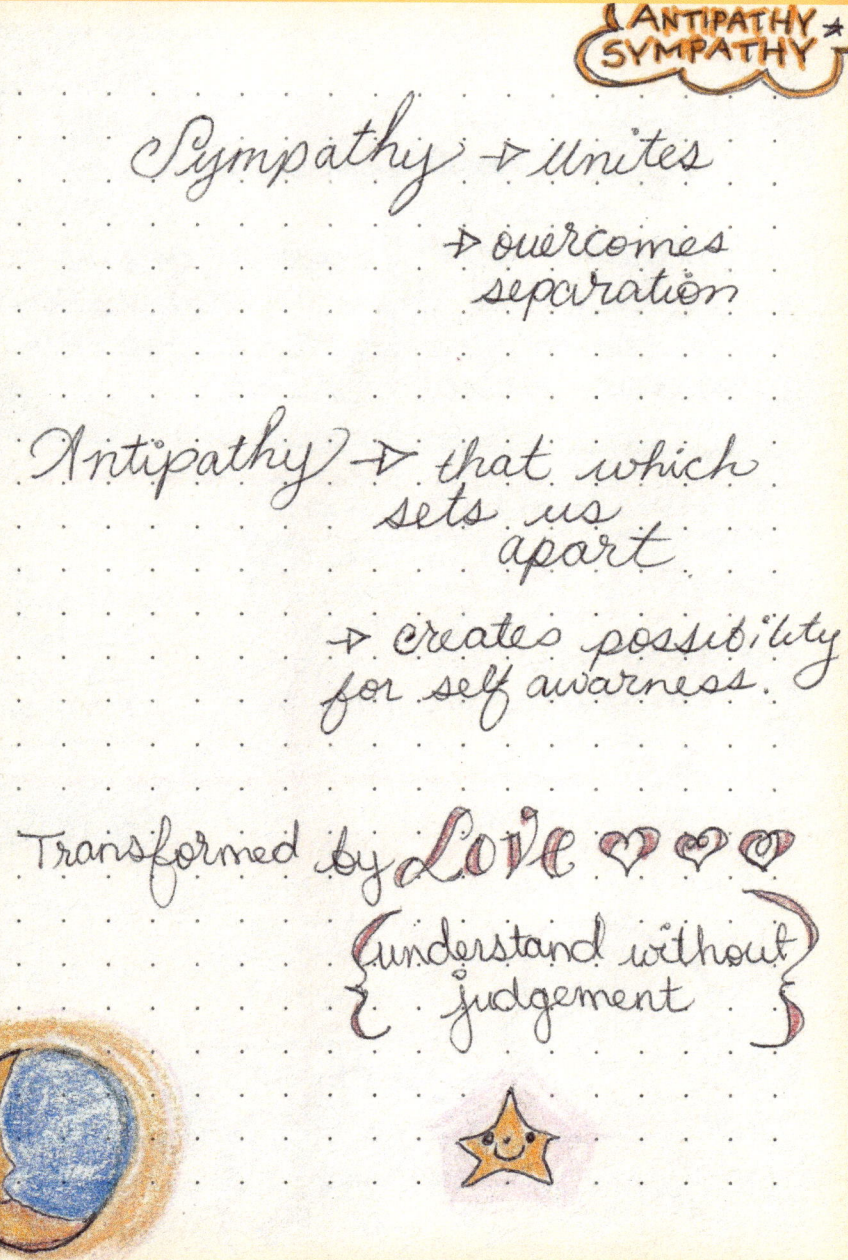

ANTIPATHY SYMPATHY ✱

Sympathy → Unites
→ overcomes separation

Antipathy → that which sets us apart
→ creates possibility for self awarness.

Transformed by *LOVE* ♡ ♡ ♡
{ understand without judgement }

Manu
   After destruction of
         Atlantis,
Manu led people from
what is now northern
Ireland to what is
now mid-China.

MIDLINE

Development often occurs dramatically over a break/vacation/holiday

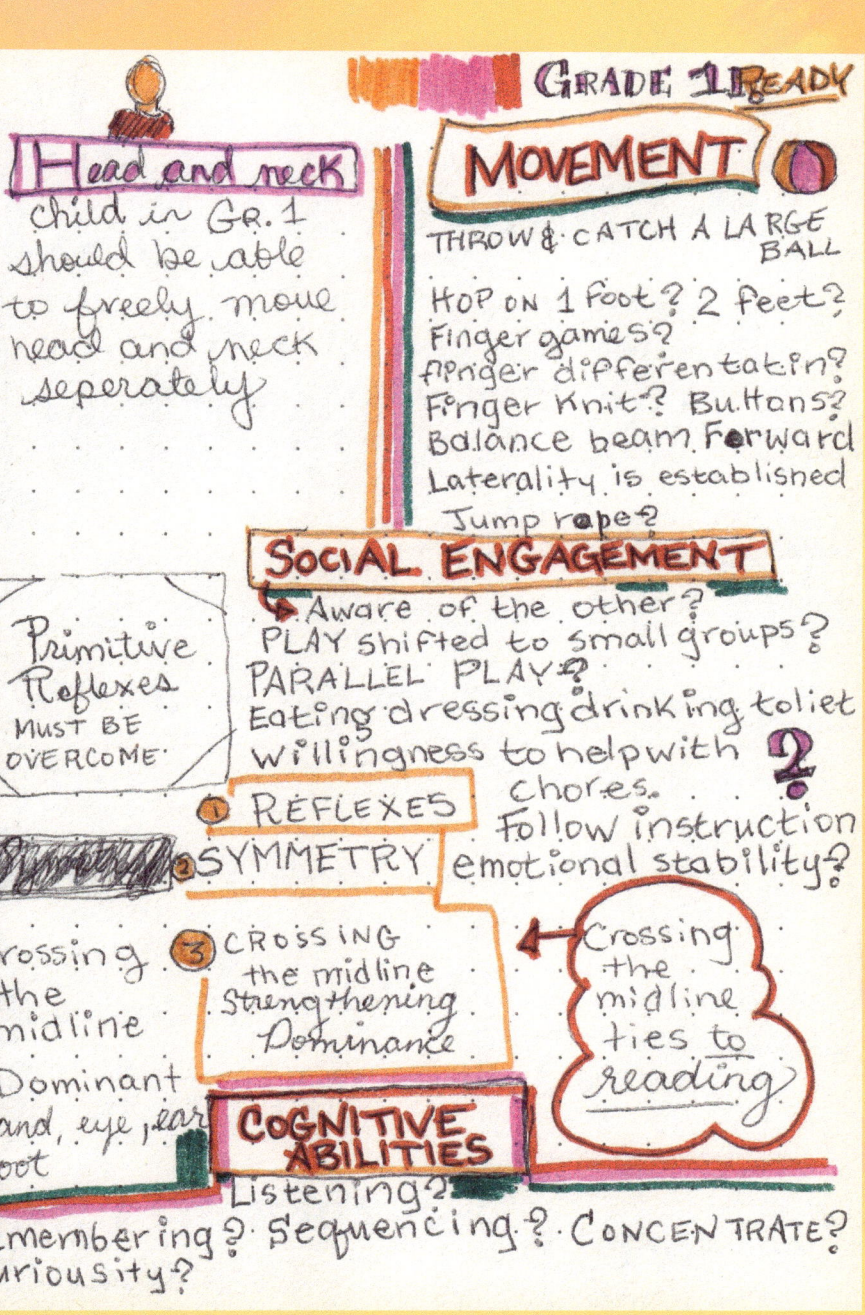

Head and neck

child in Gr. 1
should be able
to freely move
head and neck
seperately

MOVEMENT

THROW & CATCH A LARGE BALL

HOP ON 1 foot? 2 feet?
Finger games?
finger differentatin?
Finger Knit? Buttons?
Balance beam. Forward
Laterality is established
Jump rope?

SOCIAL ENGAGEMENT

→ Aware of the other?
PLAY shifted to small groups?
PARALLEL PLAY?
Eating dressing drinking toilet
willingness to help with
chores.
Follow instruction
emotional stability?

Primitive
Reflexes
MUST BE
OVERCOME

1. REFLEXES
2. SYMMETRY
3. CROSSING the midline Strengthening Dominance

→ Crossing the midline
→ Dominant hand, eye, ear, foot

Crossing the midline ties to reading

COGNITIVE ABILITIES

Listening? Sequencing? CONCENTRATE?
remembering?
Curiousity?

Home Surrondings

How to look after the home space.

★ADVENT

means anticipation, preparation, fresh, new birth, turning of Light, Clean

BLUE

Inward Quiet
virtue of the month
Guard your toungue

4ᵀᴴ Sunday before Christmas   1ˢᵗ Candle

At GRADE **6** we can ask for more input from children

An | out breath | time. Stories support!

Advent Spiral has nativity Story in it. Angel is there to help.

Apple is
→ Apple Lantern (symbol of humanity.)

ARCHANGEL ☆
GABRIEL

Ideal time to teach VOWELS!

ST. Nicholas Dec. 6
St. Lucia

Advent can be a time for challenges.

GRADE
6 7 8

ask a great question to start off the Lesson!

The first light of Advent
is the light of Stones
The Light that Shines in seashells
In crystals and in bones.

Ancient
Saturn
MINERALS

The Second Light of Advent
Is the Light of Plants
Plants that reach up to the Sun
And in the breezes dance.

Ancient
Sun
PLANTS

The third light of Advent
Is the Light of beasts.
The light of warmth, of fear, of joy.
In greatest and in least.

Ancient
Moon
Animals.

The fourth light of Advent
Is the Light of Humankind
The Light of hope, of thoughts, of deeds
of Hand and heart and mind.

Ancient
Earth
Ego

forming

Circulating

metabolic

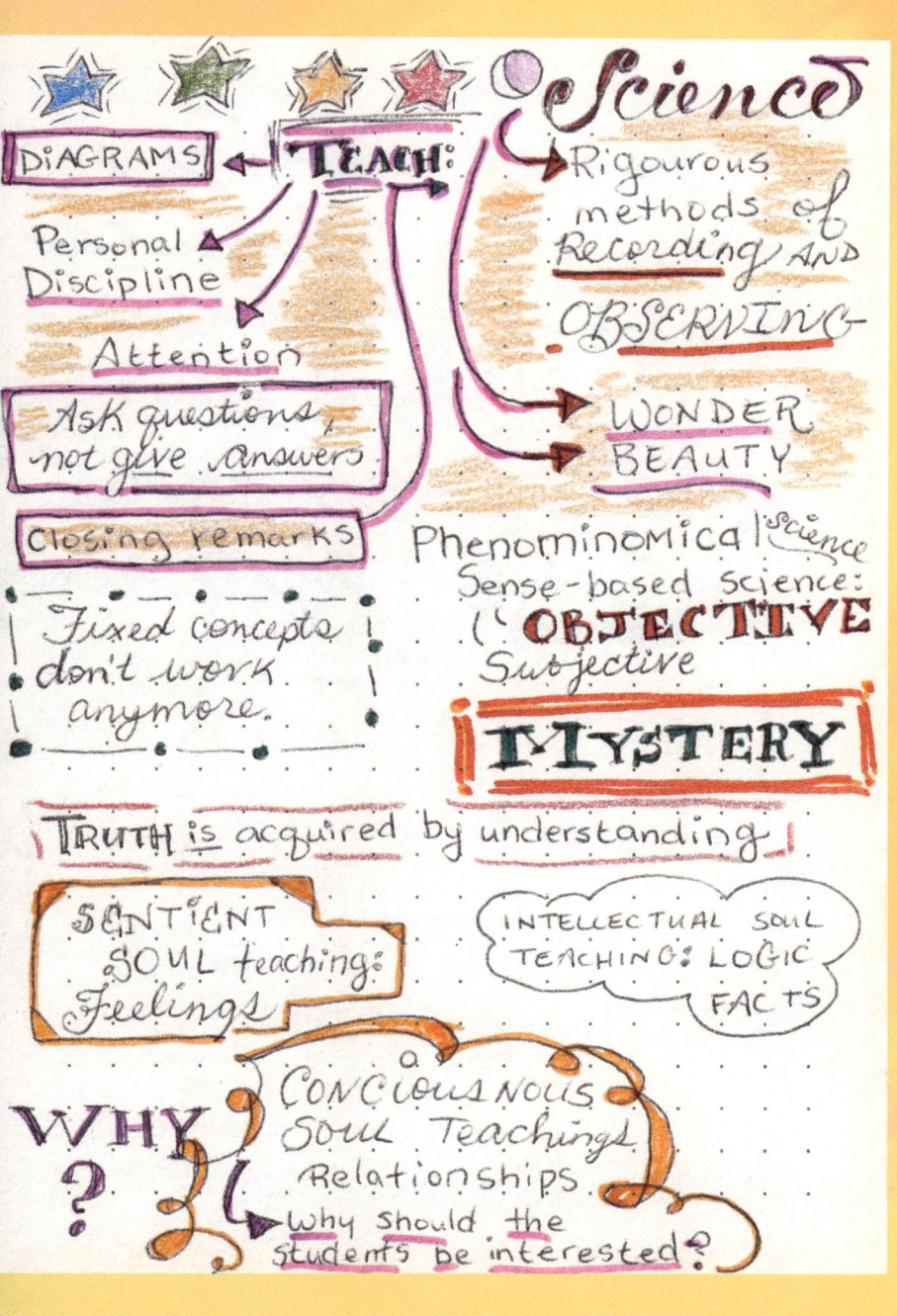

Science

DIAGRAMS ← TEACH:

Rigourous methods of Recording AND OBSERVING

Personal Discipline

Attention

Ask questions, not give answers

WONDER BEAUTY

Closing remarks

Phenominomical Science
Sense-based science:
(" OBJECTIVE
Subjective

Fixed concepts don't work anymore.

MYSTERY

TRUTH is acquired by understanding

SENTIENT SOUL teaching: Feelings

INTELLECTUAL SOUL TEACHING: LOGIC
FACTS

WHY?

a CONCIOUSNOUS SOUL Teachings Relationships
Why should the students be interested?

GR.6 : Geology
Physics

CHARLES KOVACS

GR.7 : Astronomy

INORGANIC Chemistry

LIME

CAMERA

Physics

Camera obscura

Bicycles

mechanics

GR.8 : Meteorolo

SUGAR!

HYDROLICS

ORGANIC CHEMISTRY

Electricity is esoteric

GR.6 Physics (tribo).

-▷Electricity static electricity (best for dry times)
magnetism attraction repulsion, Lodestone

-▷Acoustics: Chladney plate; instruments.
          (Relationship between sound
               and movement)
*

-▷OPTICS: (visual experiences)
          Lightness, brightness, colour

-▷Thermal (feeling objects around   the room)
  physics ▷Soudering

          -▷ Biographies of SCIENTESTS

SCIENCE

In grade 6 begin to write less for the students

* { 4 week Science Block }

DAY ① Experiment
DAY ② REVIEW. SOME NOTES
DAY ③ WRITING

INORGANIC CHEMISTRY: MINERALS

Hydrochloric Acid
NEVER ADD WATER

Find something to draw students in.

Sensible Physics Teaching
= D'ALEO
= ADLEGLASS

ORGANIC Chemistry: PLANTS
KITCHEN CHEMISTRY

Feeling ★ Experiment
WILLING ★ Discussion Description
THINKING ★ writing closing remarks.

GR.7 Physics

Thermal, Optics, electrical, mechanics

Thermal physics: Solids and Gases
Expansion, Contraction
Gaskets between solids

WATER
$4° \rightarrow 0° \rightarrow 4°$
water expands
at these
temperatures

Archimedes thermometer

farheheit to Celsius

$F \rightarrow C$

$C = (F - 32) \times \frac{5}{9}$

$C \rightarrow F$

$F = (C \times \frac{9}{5}) + 32$

$F = 77°F$

$C = (77 - 32)$

$C = \frac{45}{1} \times \frac{5}{9}$

$C = \frac{225}{9}$

$C = 25$

Cartesian
Diver

ARCHIMEDES
PRINCIPLE
water
displacement
Bathtub
incident

Science LANGUAGE

Be aware of Language.

DON'T USE
↳ Light
Heat
electricity
} NOT THINGS!!

Shadow is not "a thing"

Astronomy

↳ Heliocentric   ★ Celestial Dome
Geocentric   ★ Horizon
                   (greek for boundary

Begin
Go out and observe the sky in one spot

Astronomy: C.R. MIRBIT Book

EXPERIMENT

Redo experiments only to verify.
not because someone didn't pay attention
If experiments "Fail", redo with "new conditions." There is no Failure.

The Heart

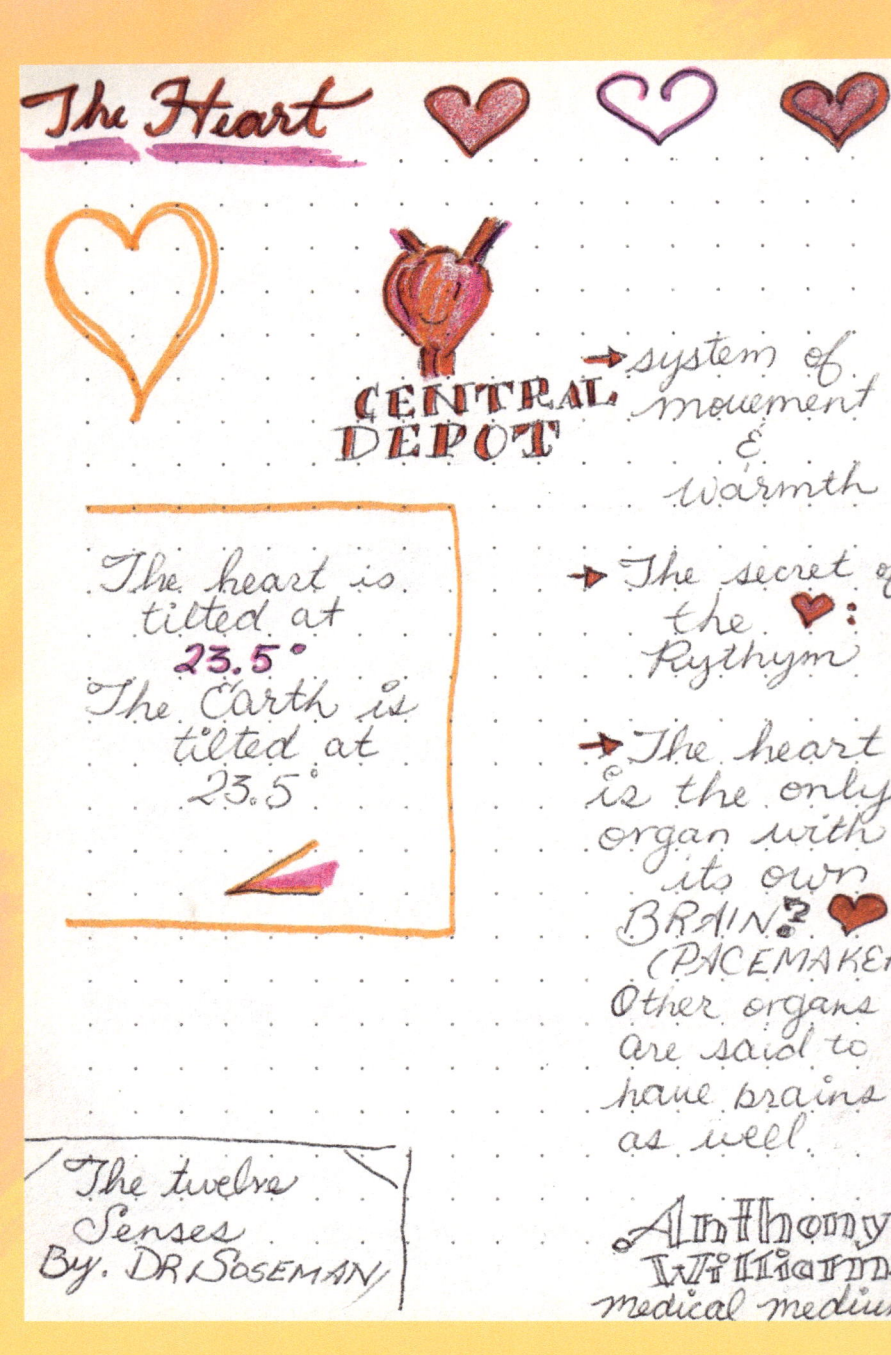

CENTRAL DEPOT

→ system of movement & warmth

→ The secret of the 🧡: Rythym

→ The heart is the only organ with its own BRAIN? 🧡 (PACEMAKER) Other organs are said to have brains as well.

The heart is tilted at **23.5°**
The Earth is tilted at 23.5°

The twelve Senses
By. DR SOSEMAN

Anthony Williams
medical medium

Set up science presentations beautifully

⭐ Clear clutter

⭐ Use a tablecloth

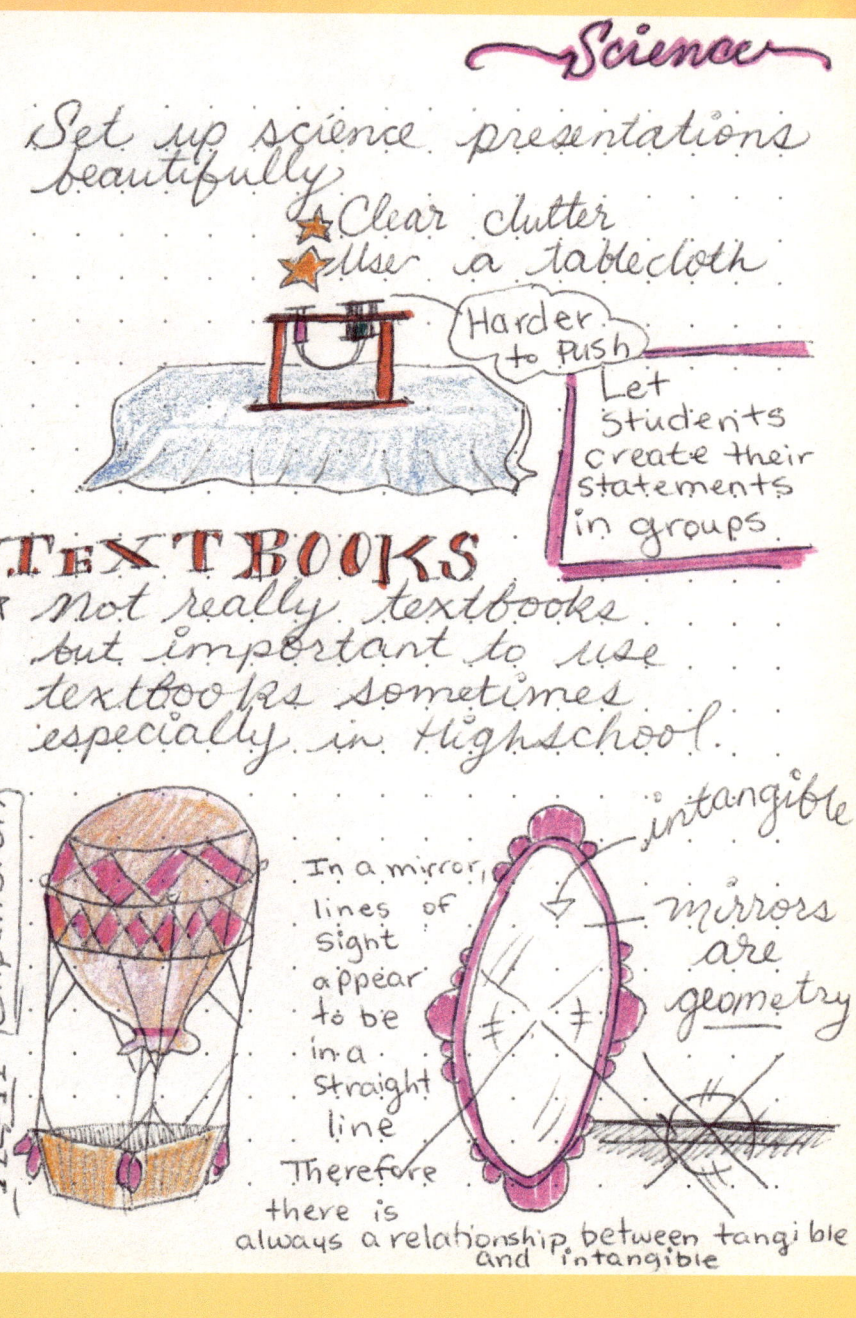

Harder to Push

Let students create their statements in groups

TEXTBOOKS

✴ Not really textbooks but important to use textbooks sometimes especially in Highschool.

HEAT Expansion

In a mirror, lines of sight appear to be in a straight line Therefore there is always a relationship between tangible and intangible

intangible

mirrors are geometry

PRISM

VERTEX UP

PRISM

A child asks a question
and ➤➤
When you don't know
the answer,

➤ Say you will
research
➤ Say to keep that
for next year, next
week, high school...

➤ Hold that thought...

♥ LOVING ♥ Authrity

- → Don't say please!
- → Don't ask, tell!▷
- → structure
- → Boundaries
- → may, not can.

PLEASE

- → Calm
- ▷ Confident
- ▷ EXPLANATIONS are important to Adolescents
- ▷ Stand in your TRUTH with teenagers.

Calm Consequences

Science

percentages!

▷ GR.8 Test at each block

→Quizzes

→ **GRADING : MARK** at school!!
  ⌐→ GR. 6: Tests (2 per year)

→ Part of main lesson on Friday is finishing the weeks works

→ teachers write their own tests
  → Have marks in sealed envelopes to open at home.

Have a Grade folder!

PLAN. night before REVEIW

↓
KEY RESOURCES

– Summer before
  → Cirriculum courses
  → Read.

AUGUST
OUTLINE BLOCKS Hand in to Faculty Chair in August!
  → Prepare our own main lesson books.

SUNDAY *prep day*

Birthday

Birthday Library
▷ ask the child to bring a book for the school / classroom library
  Give a gift on their birthday.

★ Birthday Circle

★ Birthday Poem

★ Line up by birthday

★

Teacher to studer
pp write a letter to
me explaining wha
you will do, how i
will benefit
yourself and
the class. 99

stag
Stge
stage

main Lesson
or
Circle time
(early childhood)
The ♥ heartbeat
of the class.

EARLY
CHILDHOOD
Lead and they
will follow

GRADES
form the class
into a group
soul

TRANSITIONS
Stage 1:
how quick?
2: how quiet?
: Time them
4: competition

ACTIVE
transitions
clapping

BIG
transitions
song which is
well known
sing it, everything
done by the end
of the song.

Imagination

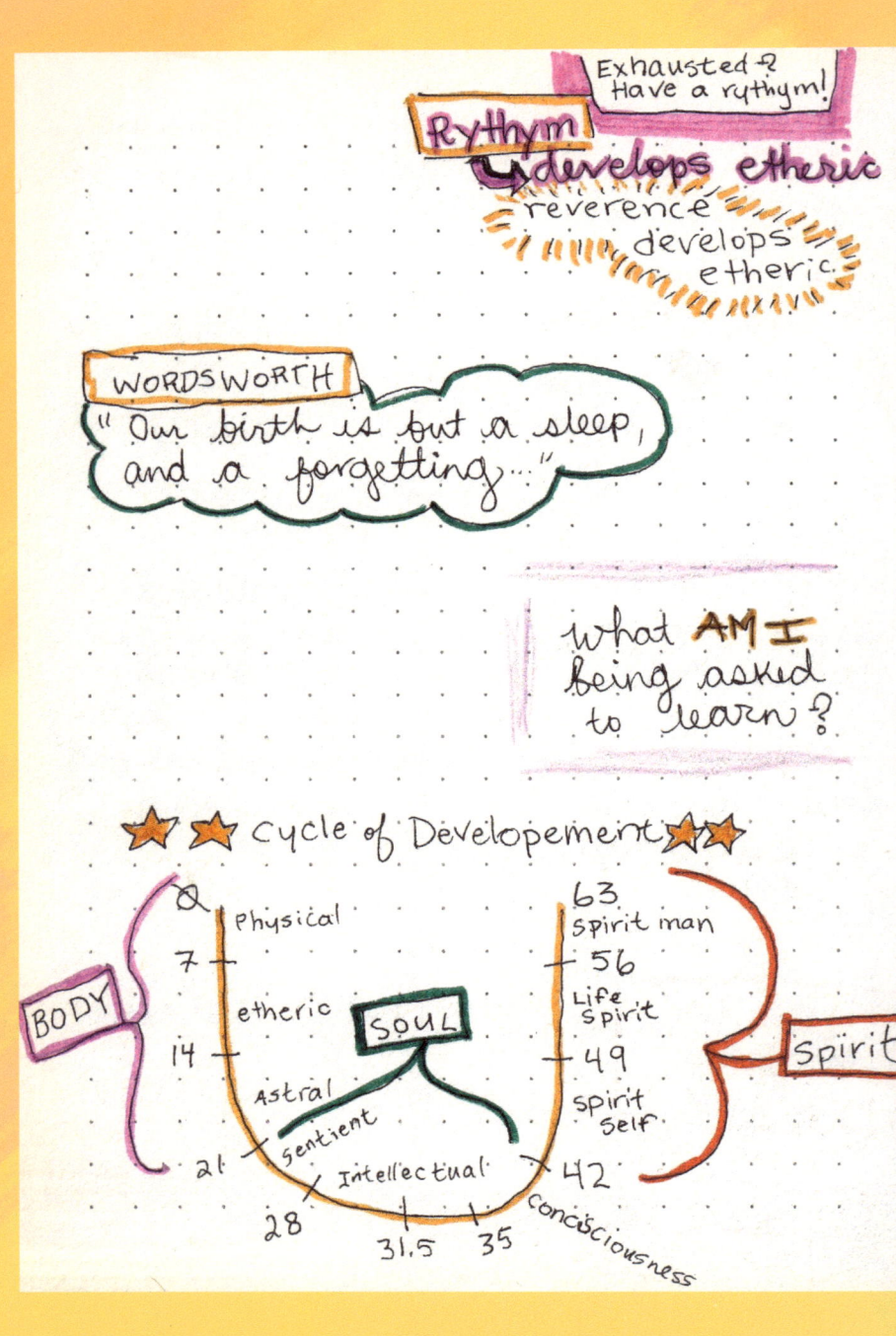

Exhausted?
Have a rythym!

Rythym develops etheric

reverence develops etheric

WORDSWORTH

"Our birth is but a sleep,
and a forgetting..."

what AM I
being asked
to learn?

⭐⭐ cycle of Developement ⭐⭐

BODY

0 — Physical
7 —
     etheric
14 —
21 — Astral
     sentient

SOUL

28   Intellectual
     31.5   35   conciousness

63 spirit man
56
Life
spirit
49
spirit
self
42

Spirit

☀ ◑ BIOGRAPHY ☆

SPIRIT REALM
spirit — spiritual science
thinking
soul — Feeling — psychology
Willing
body — biology

PHYSICAL REALM

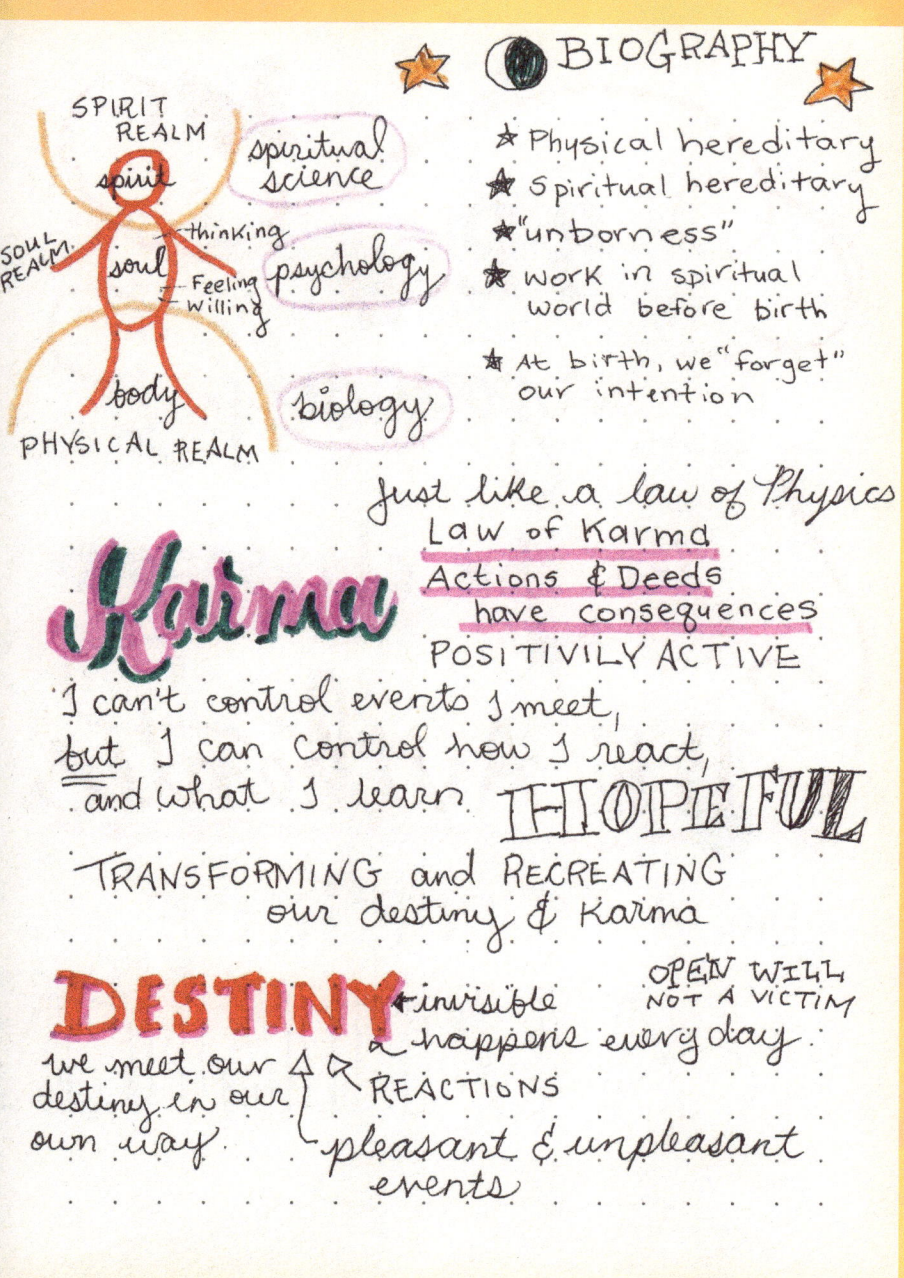

* Physical hereditary
* Spiritual hereditary
* "unbornness"
* Work in spiritual world before birth
* At birth, we "forget" our intention

Just like a law of Physics
Law of Karma
Actions & Deeds have consequences
POSITIVILY ACTIVE

Karma

I can't control events I meet,
but I can control how I react,
and what I learn.   HHOPEFUL

TRANSFORMING and RECREATING
our destiny & Karma

DESTINY ←invisible   OPEN WILL
         ↳ happens every day.   NOT A VICTIM

we meet our ↱ ↰ REACTIONS
destiny in our ⟩
own way.   ↳ pleasant & unpleasant
              events

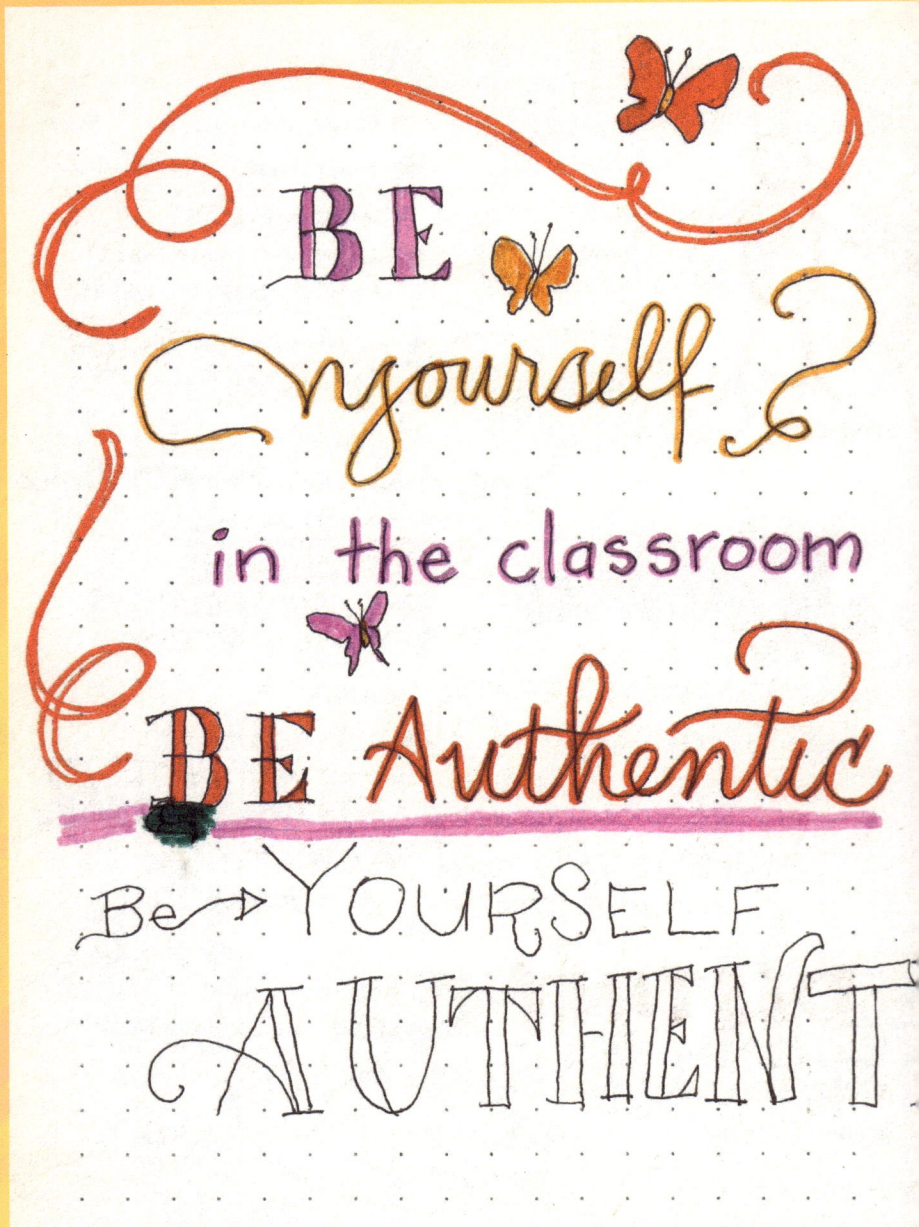

KARMA

Have <u>tension</u> between what you <u>KNOW</u> and what you <u>UNDERSTAND</u>

Attavistic

Strive

C

ETHERIC CHANGE

Long term change

★ HABITS — *Change in a habit life*

★ CHARACTER

★ TEMPERAMENT

★ *change in memory*

Listening is an act of Love

Meditation
for teachers

RYTHYM

Ruckshau
⭐ Learning to ⭐ THINK BACKWARDS

Selfawareness
Reflection

⭐ verses are CAFFIENE for our etheric!

Verses
① understand verse
② memorize
③ play it
④ find a moment of inner emptyness.

ALLOW the Verses to work on you!

MORNING
1 work with a verse
2 path of venerat-ion. Listen sound to SOUL.

CARRY veneration FOR THE DAY → Day

NIGHT
Learn to see yourself as a stranger

3rd person OBSERVATION
→ OMNIPRESENT narrator

Carry the children into the night

ZZZZZZzz

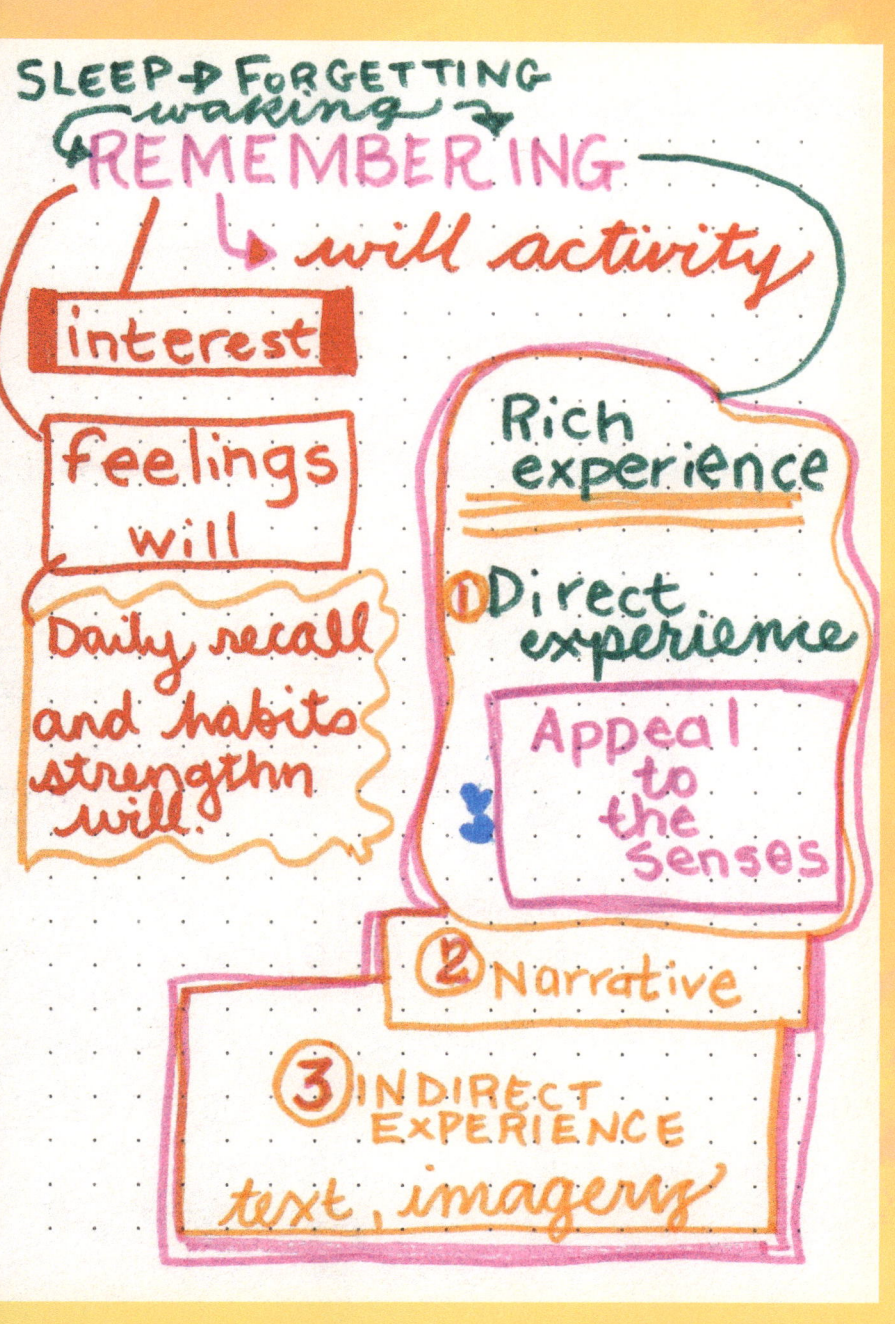

SLEEP → FORGETTING
waking →
REMEMBERING

will activity

interest

feelings
will

Daily recall
and habits
strengthn
will.

Rich
experience

① Direct
experience

Appeal
to
the
senses

② Narrative

③ INDIRECT
EXPERIENCE

text, imagery

The eye-hand painting ~~exercise~~ exercise

Painting Sequence from The Extra Lesson

for 6.5 years old and older.

any grade, over six weeks

<u>monday morning</u>

1st Lesson: BLUE

Singular motion from left to right

2ND : Red

3RD : BLUE - Top
Red - Bottom

4th : BLUE ⎫ Alternating
Red ⎭

At this time teacher may go hand over childs hand to ensure left to right

5th : BLUE: straight
Red: wavy

6TH : BLUE - wavy
Red - straight

DRY PAPER

November, before march break,
3x per year
once per term

PAINTING

★ *painting*
  Done in silence

★ Paint on opposite
  side of dominant
  hand

★ Have painting → children
  helpers   follow first
               child in row

① children stand
② Push in chair
③ Pick up boards
④ teacher sing
⑤ Place wet
  paper on board

❝ I will know we are ready to proceed
  When paintbrushes are resting on
  spongues and hands are folded in laps ❞

Rainbow Bridge Song

Here we go,
to and fro, over the
rainbow bridge we go.
down to Earth
Colours we bring
Sharing the light
So we may sing

❝ Add initials
  in lower
  right corner ❞
  with end of
  paint brush ❞

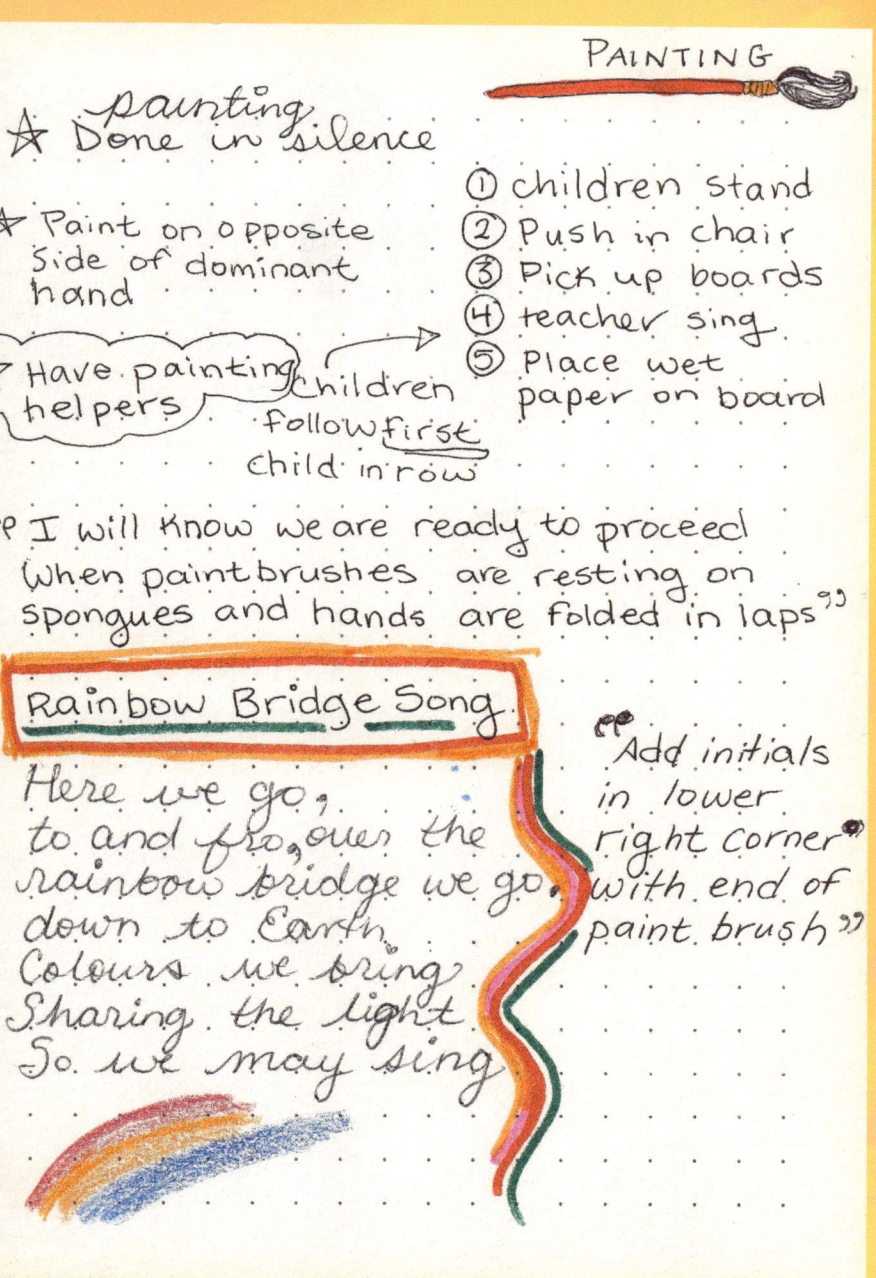

PAINTING

Help me angels of the Light
with tender care to paint aright
the colours which in me arise
Bring down to Earth from out
              of the sky

From out of my heart I too
              will bring
The colours of the rainbow ring

The Way It Is

There's a thread you follow. It goes among

things that change. But it doesn't change.

People wonder about what you are pursuing.

You have to explain the thread.

But often it is hard for others to see.

While you hold it you can't get lost.

Tragedies happen; people get hurt

or die; you suffer and get old.

Nothing you do can stop time's unfolding.

You don't ever let go of the thread.

William Stafford

Etheric Body

Brain Developement |

Etheric umbullical card to mother

LIFE FORCE

ETHERIC BODY

GROWTH
Energy
Bounce

A HABIT body

Routine
Soothes
&
Builds
Rythym

PROTECTIVE MATERNAL Sheth sheilds Etheric body

children have physical memory until teeth change

★ Recall memory is a sign of the Etheric body Free-ing

6 BEFORE Easter

6 EASTERS BEFORE GRADE ONE

The enviroment shapes the physical BODY through GOODNESS

★ GOODNESS
★ WARMTH
★ SENSORY Stimulation

Pink is Complimentary for Children.

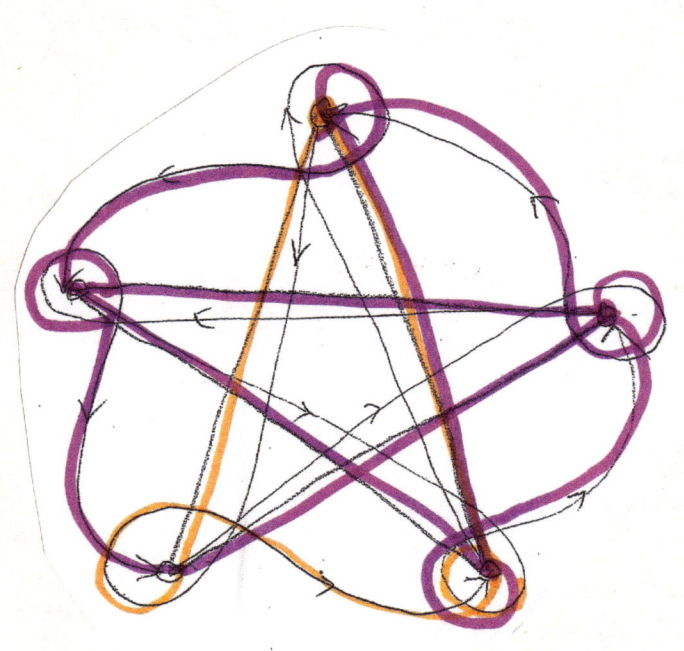

GOLDEN
CIRCLE

IN THE WOMB,
out of an
Ocean of ETHERIC

ETHERIC the physical
begins to form

wrinkles are a manifestation of Etheric receding

Physical body is Born, and we can work on it.
nourish the Baby

nourish the Soul
Etheric body is born at the Change of teeth.

→ memory
→ feeling

Etheric body is open for Shaping

BEAUTY
Veneration
Imagery
Pictures

Etheric Body understands Pictures

NOURISH ETHERIC
Fairytales and Fables

Magic
GRADE 1→8
Feeling is very important in GRADE 8

Lets return to our desk like STORKS

walk like mice

Tools for the Pedagogical BASKET

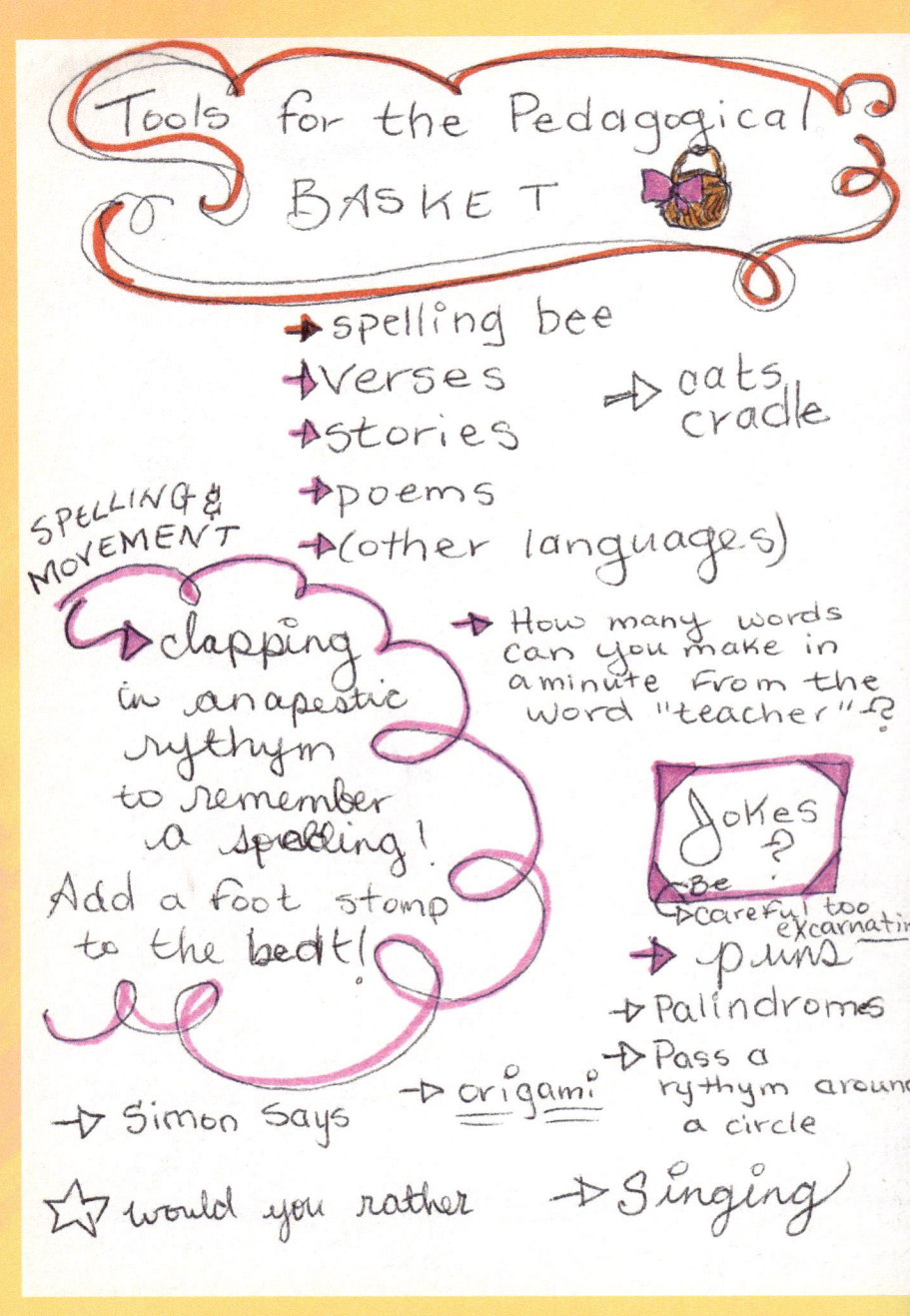

→ spelling bee
↓ Verses
↑ Stories   → cats cradle
↑ poems
↑ (other languages)

SPELLING & MOVEMENT

→ clapping
in an apestic
rythym
to remember
a spelling!

Add a foot stomp
to the beat!

→ How many words
can you make in
a minute from the
word "teacher"?

Jokes
?
→ Be
→ careful too
excarnatin
→ puns

↓ Palindromes

→ origami

→ Pass a
rythym around
a circle

→ Simon Says

☆ would you rather   → Singing

Wet on Wet painting

Paper

RAG

> wet the
> SMOOTH SIDE
> first

↑ SPONGE

↑ BRUSH

Reflect not React

> make INDIGO
> by adding a touch of
> yellow to
> the BLUE

- single colours
- Blend
- Contrast
- Polarity
- Complementary
- Primary
  Secondary
  (tertiary)

Etheric moisture

yellow paint "moves" Joyfully

Blue paint puts up a Boundary. STATIC Draws us Down / in.

Red has heat, but a stop sign as well.

The Song of the Sun

I give light
Light give I

I give warmth
Warmth give I.

I give life
Life give I

This is the song
of the Sun

The sun's song
is this.

Teacher

teachers ego must Fill the room

→ Centred and Still

move around the Classroom while posing questions

THEN → students project Voice!

INSTEAD of marks on the Board, Corners, Hallways etc.

AUTORITÉ AFFIRMATIVE LOVING AUTHORITY

Positive Discipline

This student is sitting so nicely and ready for the lesson.

row 1, or Deborah all the way to you may go get your snack.

Cui Ting

❤ ↔ ❤ heart to heart

IF a student is a clown, ask to see them later. Tell Them you would love for

In order to not have students correct each other, suggest they say "I would like to add...."

CLASSROOM CULTURE
Teachers can ask: "who would like to add...."

good behavior.

them to participate in snack right away, create a secret signal with them to signal you have seen their

Them to be able to

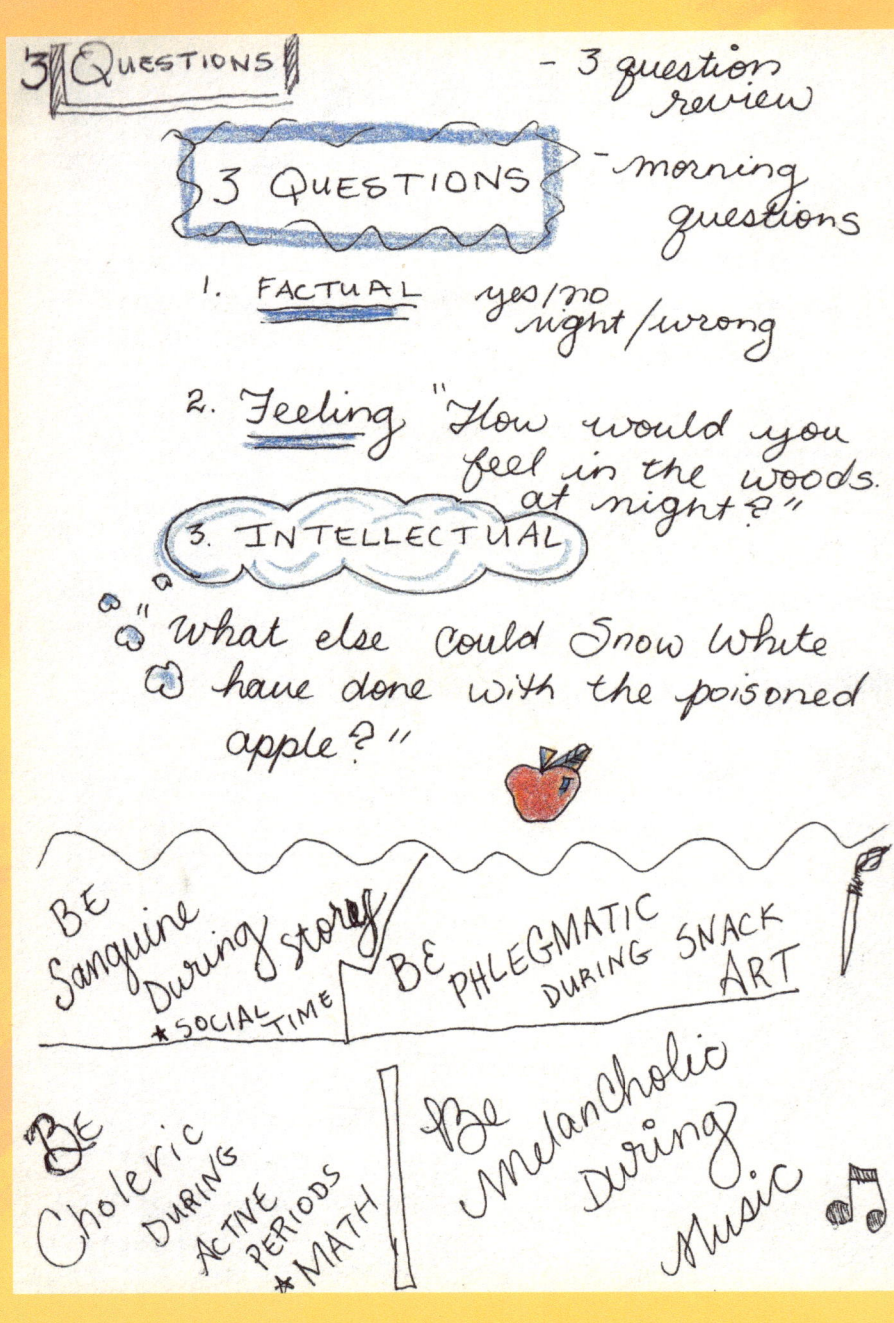

3 QUESTIONS

- 3 question review
- morning questions

3 QUESTIONS

1. FACTUAL yes/no right/wrong

2. Feeling "How would you feel in the woods at night?"

3. INTELLECTUAL

"What else could Snow White have done with the poisoned apple?"

BE Sanguine During story
*SOCIAL TIME

BE PHLEGMATIC DURING SNACK ART

BE Choleric DURING ACTIVE PERIODS *MATH

Be Melancholic During Music

Temperments

TOOLS for this LIFE.
{ Result from Previous incarnations }

Everybody has all **4**

Ancient greeks preceived the 4 temperments

TEMPERMENTS

SANGUINE

PHLEGMATIC

MELANCHOLIC

CHOLERIC

GRADE 4/5, temperaments become less prominent

Find a Balance of <u>all</u> **4**

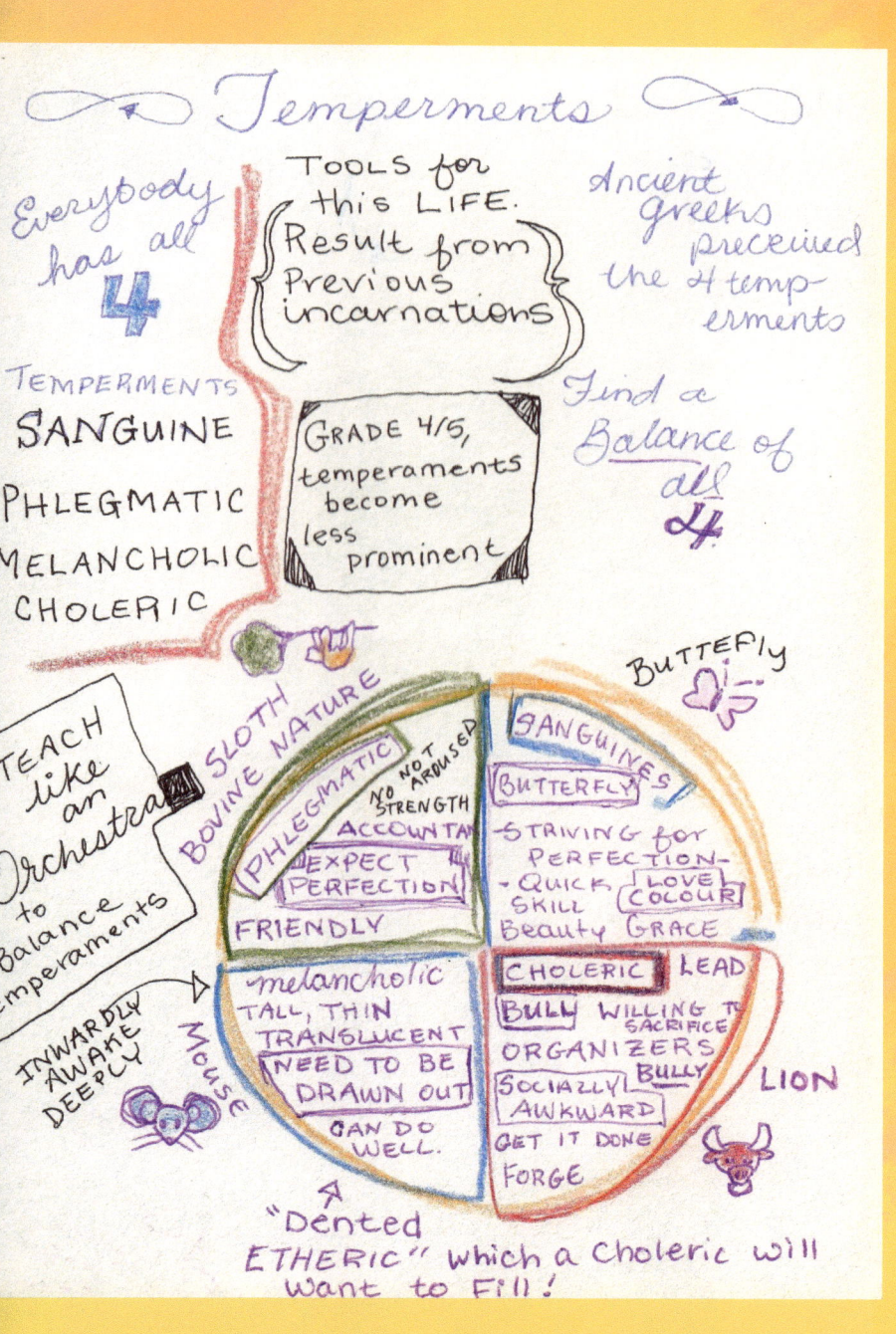

TEACH like an Orchestra to Balance Temperments

SLOTH BOVINE NATURE

INWARDLY AWAKE DEEPLY

PHLEGMATIC
NO NOT AROUSED
STRENGTH
ACCOUNTANT
EXPECT PERFECTION
FRIENDLY

SANGUINES
BUTTERFLY
- STRIVING for PERFECTION-
- QUICK SKILL
LOVE COLOUR
Beauty GRACE

BUTTERFLY

melancholic
TALL, THIN
TRANSLUCENT
NEED TO BE DRAWN OUT
CAN DO WELL.

Mouse

CHOLERIC   LEAD
BULL   WILLING TO SACRIFICE
ORGANIZERS
SOCIALLYL AWKWARD   BULLY
GET IT DONE
FORGE

LION

"Dented ETHERIC" which a Choleric will want to Fill!

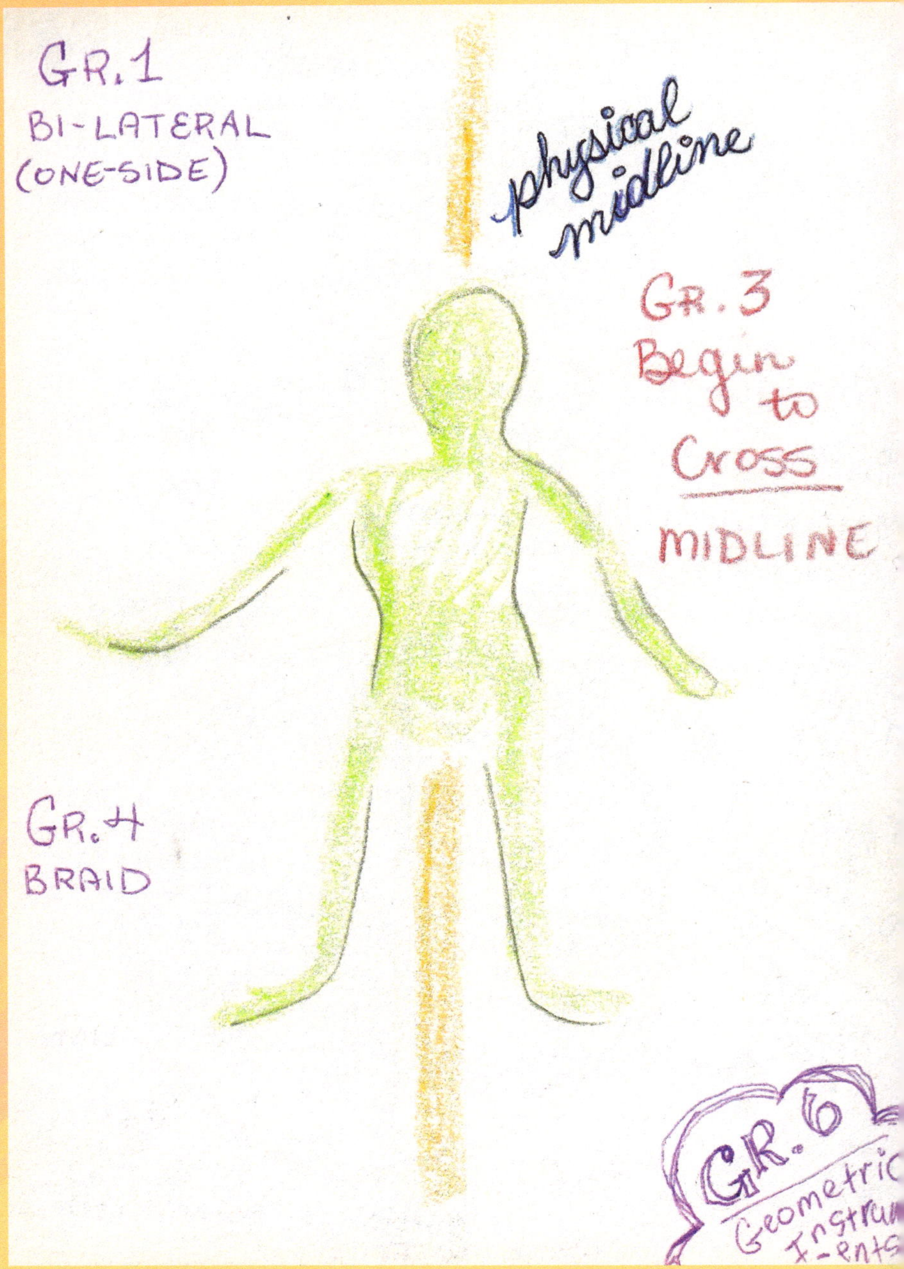

GR.1
BI-LATERAL
(ONE-SIDE)

physical midline

GR.3
Begin
to
Cross
MIDLINE

GR.4
BRAID

GR.6
Geometric
Instrum-
ents

FORM DRAWING

flowing, like free thought

— use this EDGE

* Choleric child will wear out crayon!

* spatial awareness

- MOVEMENT
- SPACE

* what was before and what is to come.

* standing ok, but push back chair

Re-experiencing the soul and spirit in spirit land.

* Do not go back and fix your LINES *

Flow.

- ONE form at a time
- form drawing only on the page.
- Decorate another page.
- go over in the air first

CORRECT GRIP

Strive to overcome imperfection,
However perfection is not the goal

FROM form TO FREEDOM

- GR. 3 LYRA CRAYONS

- GR. 2 switch from BLOCK to Stick.

Teach
Letters

Letters descend
from heaven
to standing on
ground (red)

STORY
↓
IMAGE
↓
LETTER

From Heaven....
to standing
on the ground

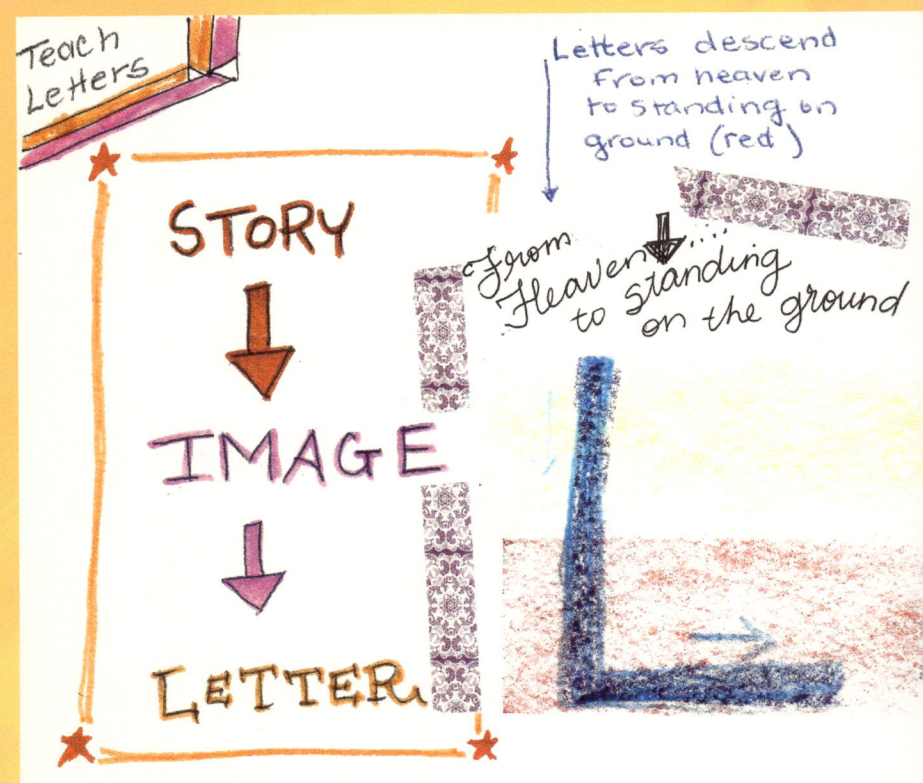

→ Draw on Blackboard with a wet mop.
→ Draw on child's back, and have
child & children guess
→ whoever sits up straight while
writing gets to where the crown for the
day.

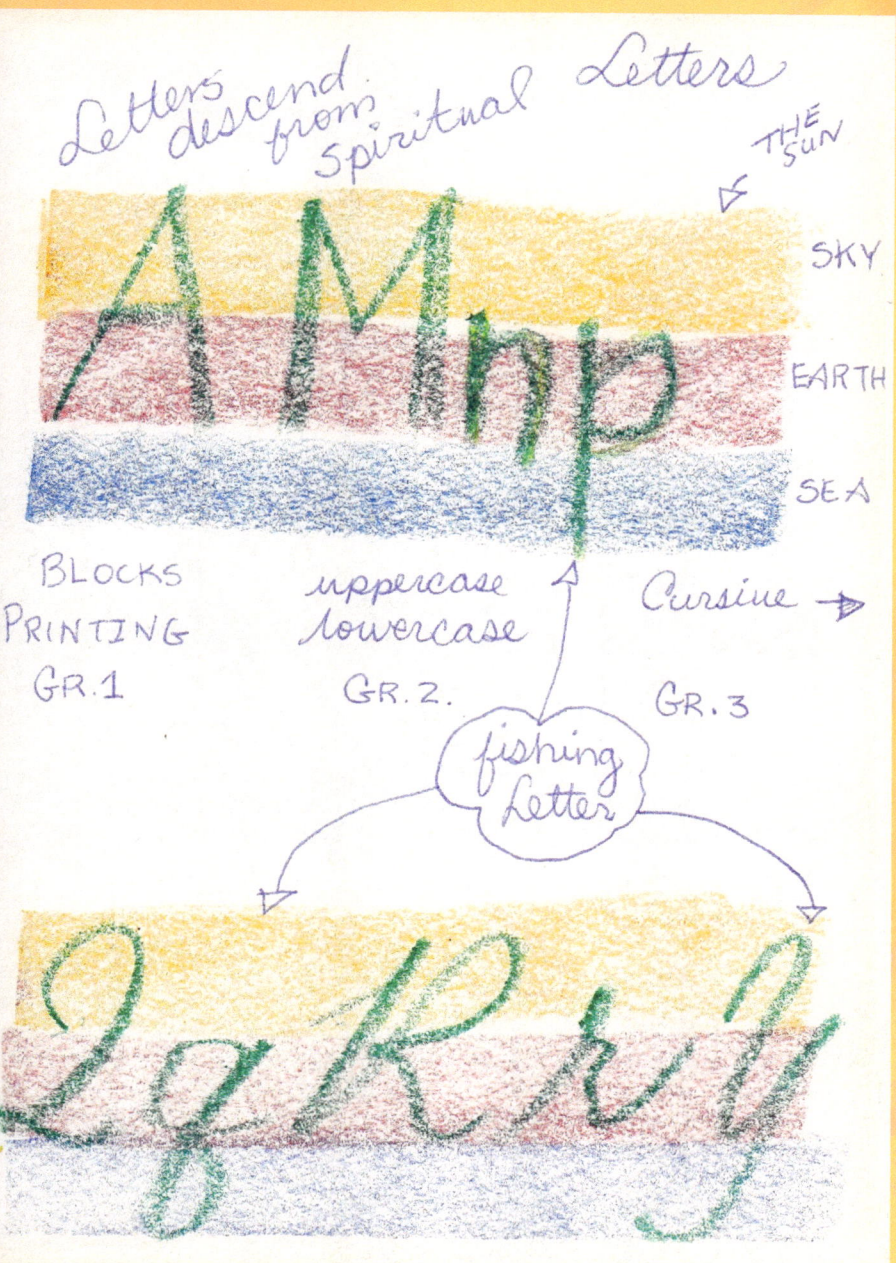

GRAMMAR

that that is is that that is
not is not is not that
      it is

Human Developement

Educate through:
↳ ARTS
↳ feeling

TRUTH

BIRTH of the "I"

21

FREEDOM

EDUCATION IS thinking + Debating.

14

BIRTH of ASTRAL

BEAUTY

LEADING, USING, LIVING IMAGES

6/7

BIRTH of Etheric

pedagogical methods

pedagogical principles

IMITATION

The Process of Incarnation

Spirit
Soul
↓
Life
Body

GOODNESS

Educate the young Child through the Body

Birth of Physical Body

KAMALOKA 2/3 RDS

Pralaya

DEVAKAAN

Doing it better next time

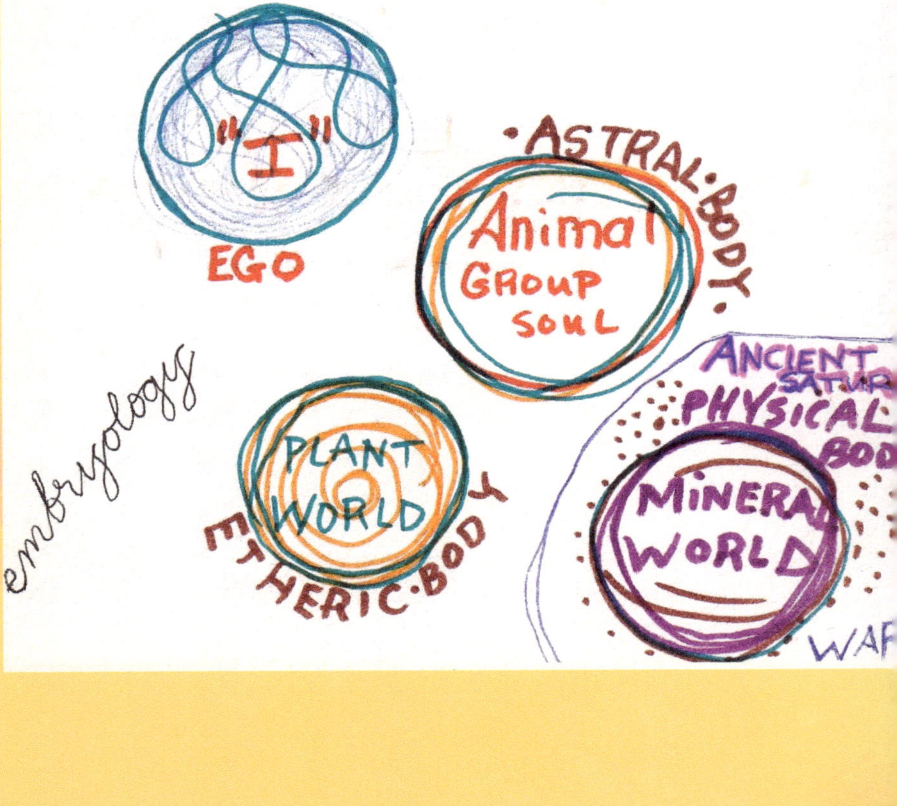

"I"

EGO

• ASTRAL • BODY •

Animal GROUP SOUL

embryology

ANCIENT SATURN

PHYSICAL BODY

PLANT WORLD

ETHERIC • BODY

MINERAL WORLD

WAR

The 3 Soul Forces

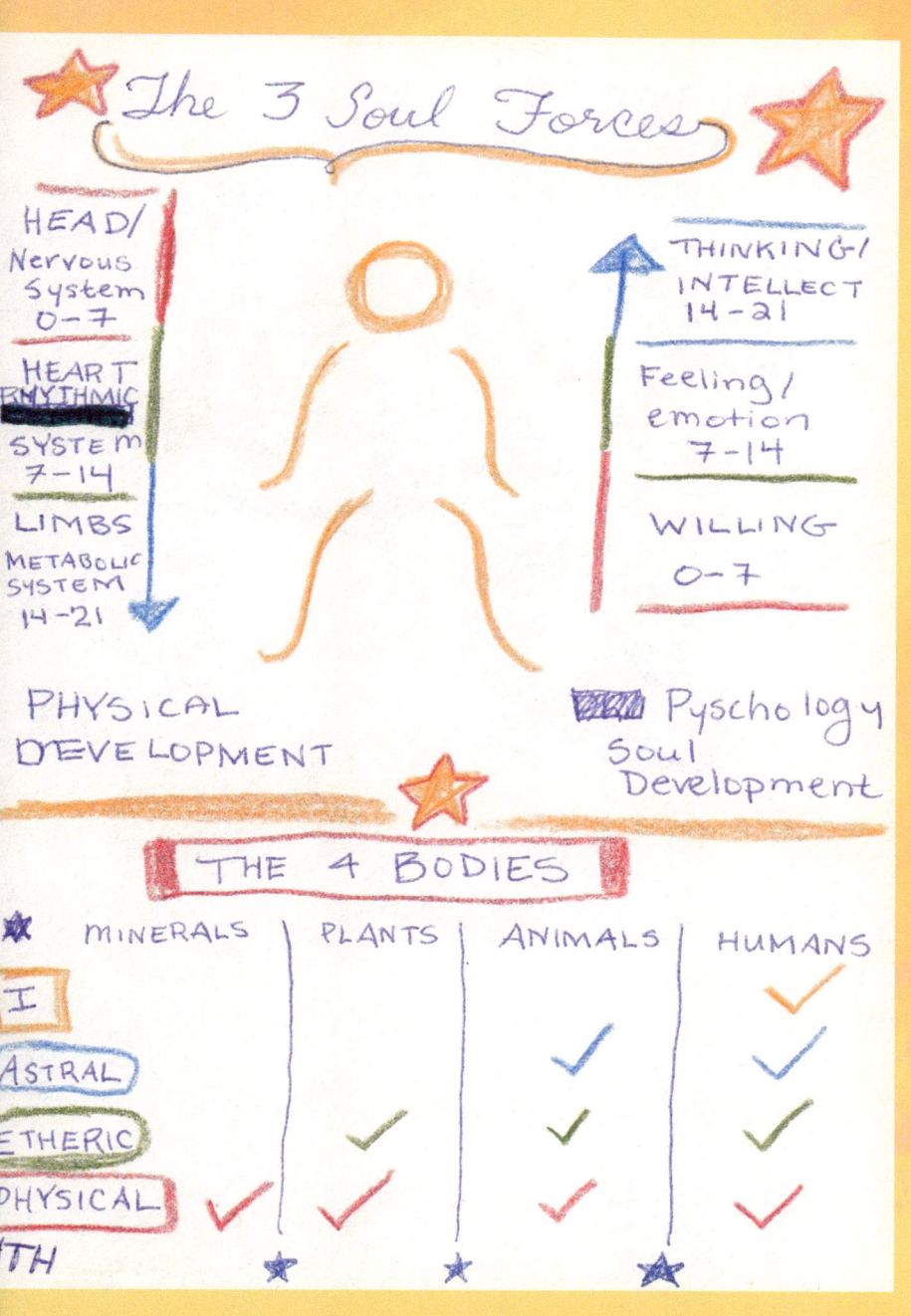

HEAD/
Nervous
System
0-7

HEART
RHYTHMIC
SYSTEM
7-14

LIMBS
METABOLIC
SYSTEM
14-21

THINKING/
INTELLECT
14-21

Feeling/
emotion
7-14

WILLING
0-7

PHYSICAL
DEVELOPMENT

Pyschology
Soul
Development

THE 4 BODIES

	MINERALS	PLANTS	ANIMALS	HUMANS
I				✓
ASTRAL			✓	✓
ETHERIC		✓	✓	✓
PHYSICAL	✓	✓	✓	✓
TH	★	★	★	

MATH WOMAN

Math Woman

M W

Difficult class of adolescences?

mr. petrast drew math woman with the children on the board every session

DESCENDING OUT OF THE Temperament Profile

SANGUINE

Fingers:
Balance
Beauty

* IN-BETWEEN

* ENERGY

OUTER NATURE

QUICK LEARNER
LOVE COLOUR

PHLEGMATIC

Fingers:
long, full
tapered

* BROAD

* PEAR SHAPED

INNER

ASLEEP
ROUTINE
OBSERVE
DETAIL

GOOD ACCOUNTANT
- focused on the
need for comfort

MELANCHOLIC

Respond to sympathy.

fingers:
long, slim
diaphenous

* Tall slim

INWARD FOCUS

pale

INNER

Slow but
ENGAGED

DRAGGING
HISTORY

SUFFERS!

EMPATHY

EASIER
ACCESS
TO
SELF
DISCIPLINE

CHOLERIC

OUTER NATURE

Fingers:
short,
broad,
work.

WHAT CAN I CHANGE

* BROAD
LEADERSHIP

* INVISIBLE
NECK

* SQUARE
HEAD

BROAD
SHOULDERS

Feet:

Three types of speech

① Direct (teaching - sit down) (DRAMATIC)

② Epic/storytelling speech (INVITING)

③ (Poetic) Lyric (SILK)

VISUAL SUPPORT for the TEMPERAMENTS

Remedial FORM DRAWING

support to sanguine children

melancholic

CHOLERIC

SANGUINES

CHOLERIC needs to add & ENCLOSE

ENCLOSE

THEN ERASE CIRCL

Black Board

SEATING PLAN

AT GR. 7, students can make their own plan, taking into account each student.

maintain seating arrangement until GR. 7.

"GROUP SOUL ENTITY"

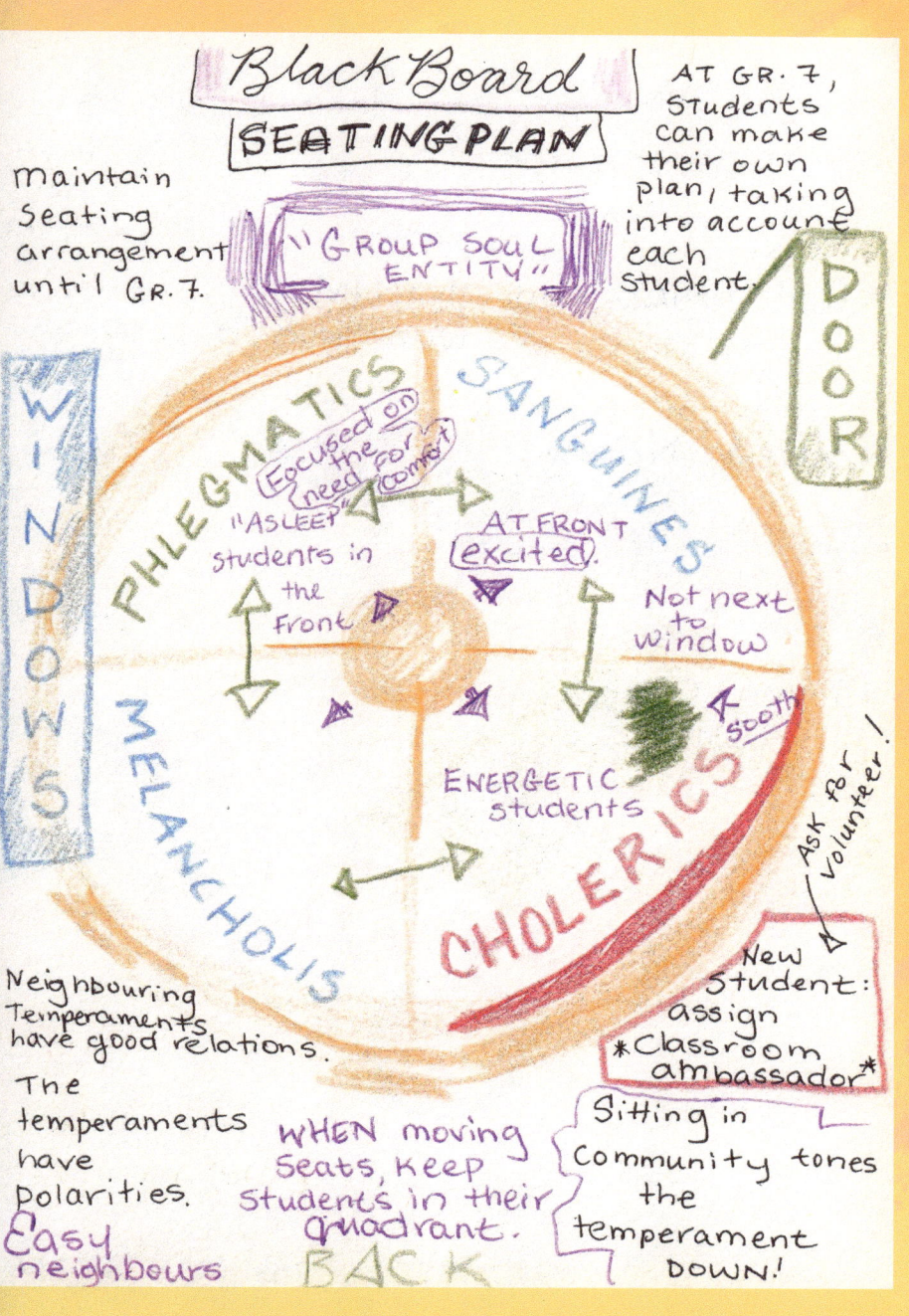

WINDOWS

DOOR

PHLEGMATICS

Focused on the need for comfort

"ASLEEP" students in the Front

SANGUINES

AT FRONT excited.

Not next to window

MELANCHOLIS

ENERGETIC students

sooth

CHOLERICS

Ask for volunteer!

New Student: assign *Classroom ambassador*

Neighbouring Temperaments have good relations.

The temperaments have polarities.

Easy neighbours

WHEN moving seats, keep students in their quadrant.

Sitting in community tones the temperament DOWN!

BACK

" TO A MOUSE " by Robert Burns

melancholic verse.

★ DAFFODILS by WILLIAM
                    WORDSWORTH

★ Alfred Noyes

★ "Breathing" Goethe

★ John Donne

★ Mary Oliver

CLASS TEACHER

"I AM LOOKING FOR STUDENTS who are ready for Snack"

what you Focus on Expands

FOCUS ON the Positive

Spend time on the playground

Deal with Bullys

Ask Both children to come.
Say, "Alana, Diego is going to recount what happened, then I would like you to repeat it back to me."

* Ask Both children to agree.
* One child tells what happened. Then the other repeats. Then ask the other child if the recount is correct.
* Repeat with other child.

→ Creating a framework for self discipline and self control

↛ Life is a process. Ever changing.

Challenges
are a
moment of
Learning

Saturn Return
28-30 years
Father time
past/Further
reflection

31-33
❤
Heart of
our
Biography

Age of Michäel
(NOW)
age of conciousness
Soul

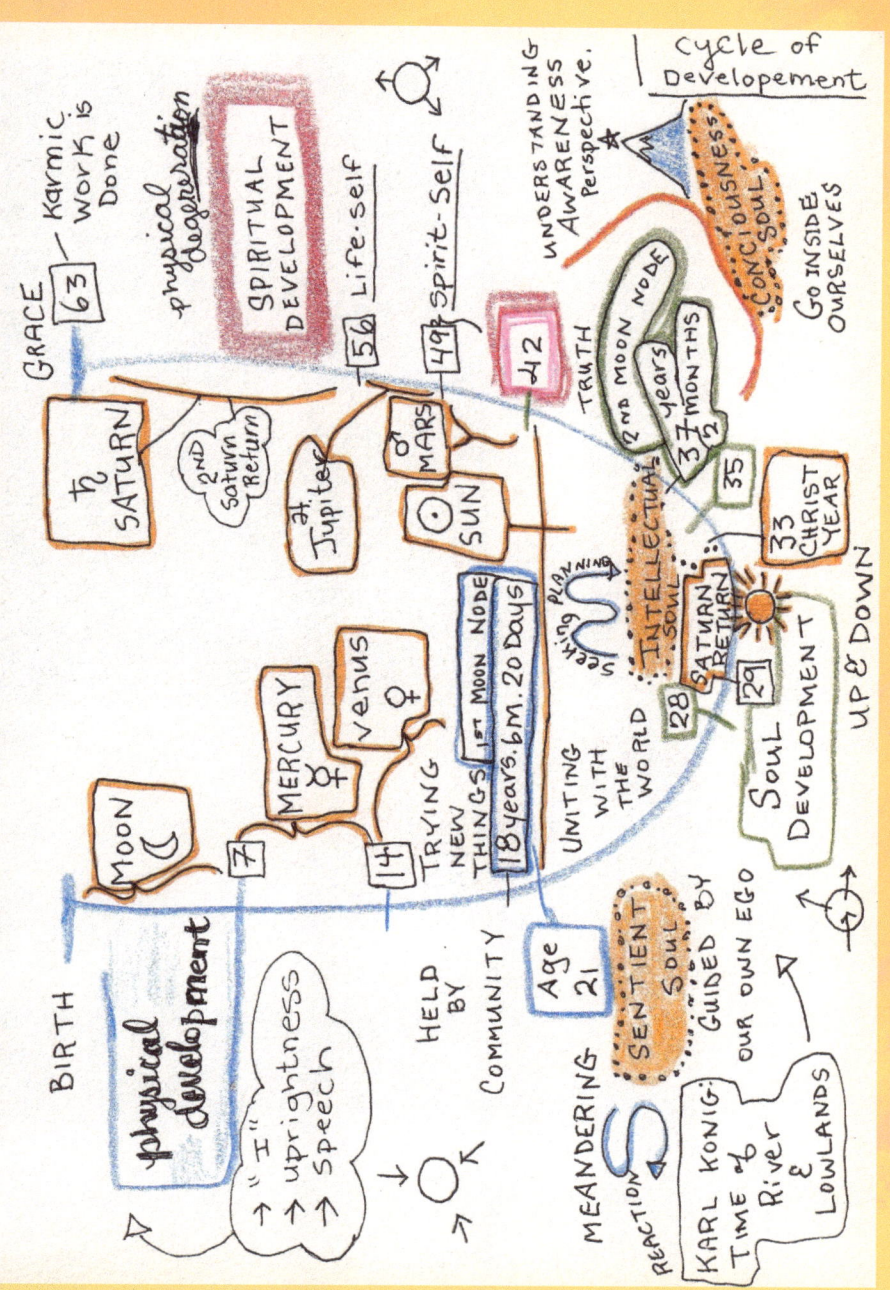

Cycle of Development

GRACE

63 — Karmic work is Done

physical degeneration

SPIRITUAL DEVELOPMENT

56 Life-self

49 Spirit-Self

42

TRUTH

UNDERSTANDING
AWARENESS
Perspective.

CONCIOUSNESS
SOUL

GO INSIDE
OURSELVES

♄ SATURN

2ND Saturn Return

♃ Jupiter

♂ MARS

☉ SUN

2ND MOON NODE
37 years
2 months

35

33 CHRIST YEAR

INTELLECTUAL SOUL

SEEKING PLANNING

SATURN RETURN

28   29

SOUL DEVELOPMENT

UP & DOWN

MOON ☽

MERCURY ☿

VENUS ♀

7

14

1st MOON NODE

18 years, 6m. 20 Days

TRYING NEW THINGS

UNITING WITH THE WORLD

Age 21

SENTIENT SOUL

GUIDED BY OUR OWN EGO

BIRTH

physical development

→ "I"
→ uprightness
→ Speech

HELD BY COMMUNITY

MEANDERING

REACTION

KARL KONIG: TIME of River & LOWLANDS

Music

Below age **9** → **pentatonic**

Concert A: 440 H · TRUE A: 432 H

A B C D E F G... → *more about intervals* THAN notes

Note of the Sun

NOTES: A, B, D, E, G,

Mood of the 5TH
FOR THE YOUNGEST CHILDREN

"NO BACK"

KINDER HARP

OPEN

TUNE

NAP TIME
before story
end of story

DIATONIC Recorder

Give a feather or bit of roving to encourage Gentle blowing

How to choose a SONG?
* SONG BOOKS
* make a round for older children

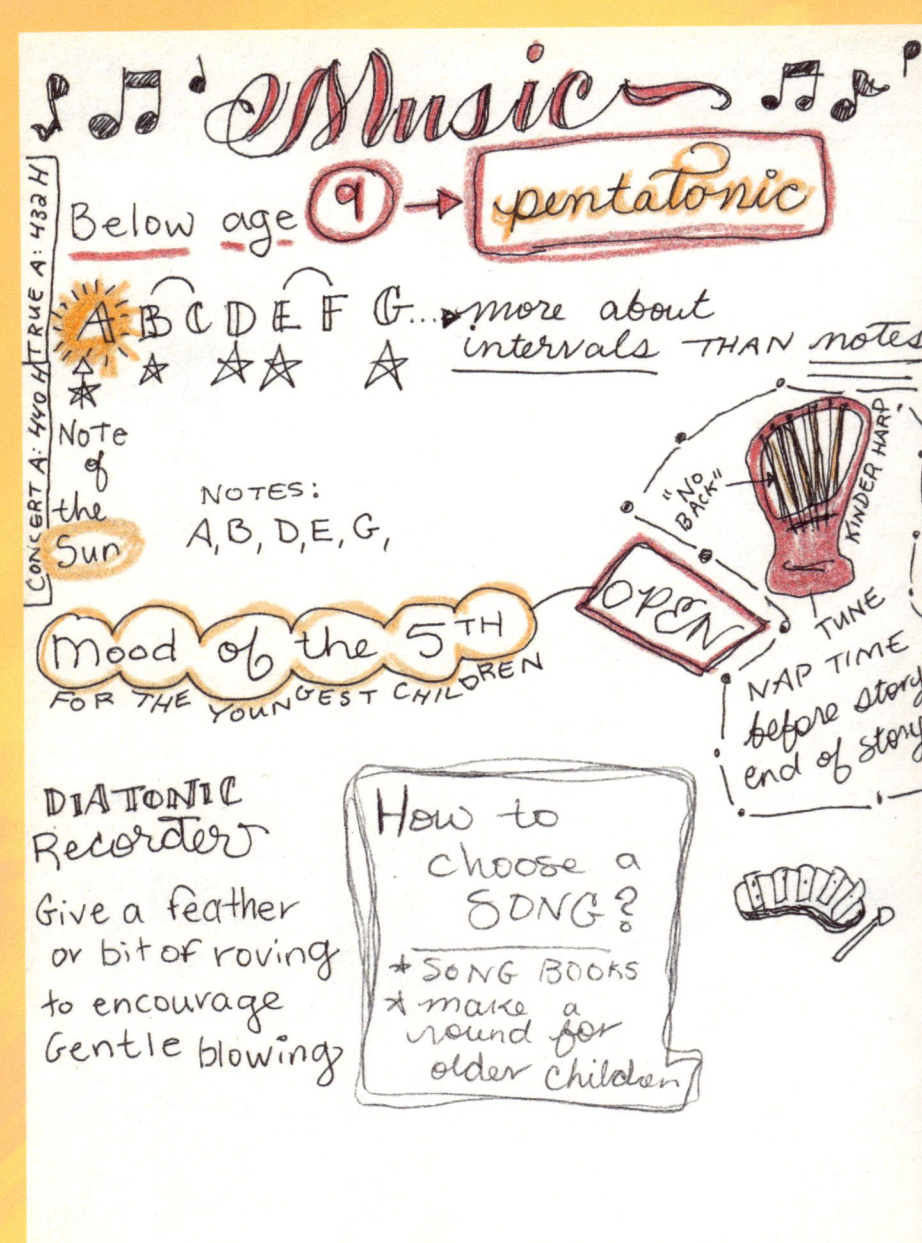

SINGING

gning gnong gnong

NG → This sound heals voice.

PLUG NOSE! ends "ng" sound.

Listen! KEY to better singing

Singing can heal! even sore throat

Teach Recorder

* have recorders in desk. Then ask students put recorder at end of desk on case.

* Then sing song.

DOWN

hold
recorder
in
down
position

POSTURE

(A) Angel with TWO WINGS

(B) Bumble "B"

(C) Letter C

(D)

(E)

(F) Funny F

(G) genie with 3 WISHES

(D)
(C) "deep C"

sun sun raindrop shhh pitter patter

Gim

Bam

Biddy Biddy

Bam

*Greeting at door.

* Teacher stands.
  * *pause*.* *look* for who is *ready*.
  I love how the window side is standing straight.

Today is Wednesday October 12

Extra main
Music
Painting

GRADE 1

Draw the jobs on the Board

→ Picture Form of jobs with intials.

GRADE 2.

Children teach each other the jobs in their free time.

CLASSROOM MANAGEMENT: ROOM CLEANING

Children have a system of classroom jobs.
→ visible jobs
→ changeable
→ week is too short.
4 weeks effective.
End of 3rd week is TRANSITION

THREE FOLDING

THEOCRACY

Religious state

Culture
Rights
Economy

FRENCH Revolution 1795

Equalité
Fraternité
Liberté

Green Snake and Beautiful LILY
GOETHE
fairy tale OF Threefolding

CULTURE
freedom
meritocracy

Economy
↳ Needs

1. roll over
2. crawl
3. Balance
4. Walk
5. Speech

The Education of The Self

Development of moral imagination

The cow has spirals

⭐ Child Development

RYTHM of
Early Childhood

① head development — BIRTH
② broaden trunk (3-5)
③ Lengthn Limbs (6-7)

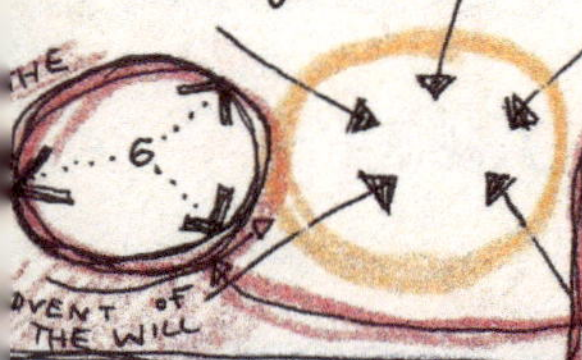

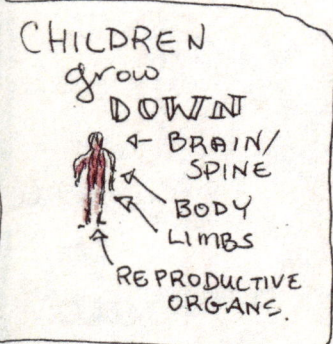
THE · 6 ·
DVENT OF
THE WILL

① Head Development (Gr. 1, 2, 3)
② Broaden (GR. 4, 5, 6)
③ Lengthn (GR. 6, 7, 8)
TRUE WILL ⟩ Beginning of HumAn CONCIOUSNESS

SELF PROGRESS

GR. 9 │ HEAD
GR. 10 │ BROADEN
GR. 11, 12 │ Lengthn

CHILDREN
grow
DOWN

← BRAIN/ SPINE
← BODY LIMBS
REPRODUCTIVE ORGANS.

GROWTH
PULSE +
⭐
SPIRAL

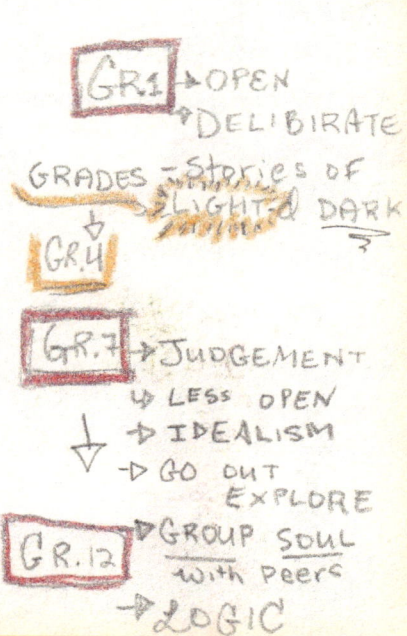

GR 1 → OPEN
→ DELIBIRATE

GRADES — Stories of LIGHT & DARK

GR. 4

GR. 7 → JUDGEMENT
↳ LESS OPEN
→ IDEALISM
→ GO OUT EXPLORE

GR. 12 → GROUP SOUL with peers
→ LOGIC

SPIRIT SOUL

LIFE BODY

What is a human being?

A Spirit Soul in a physical Body

Moral intuition

Moral Imagination

Moral Techniques

"Freedom"

INDIVIDUALISM

Ethical

MORAL IMAGINATION ... DESTINY

MORAL Imagination in teaching

WHOLE

⇩

PART

Reverence & Respect is NUTRITION for ANGELS

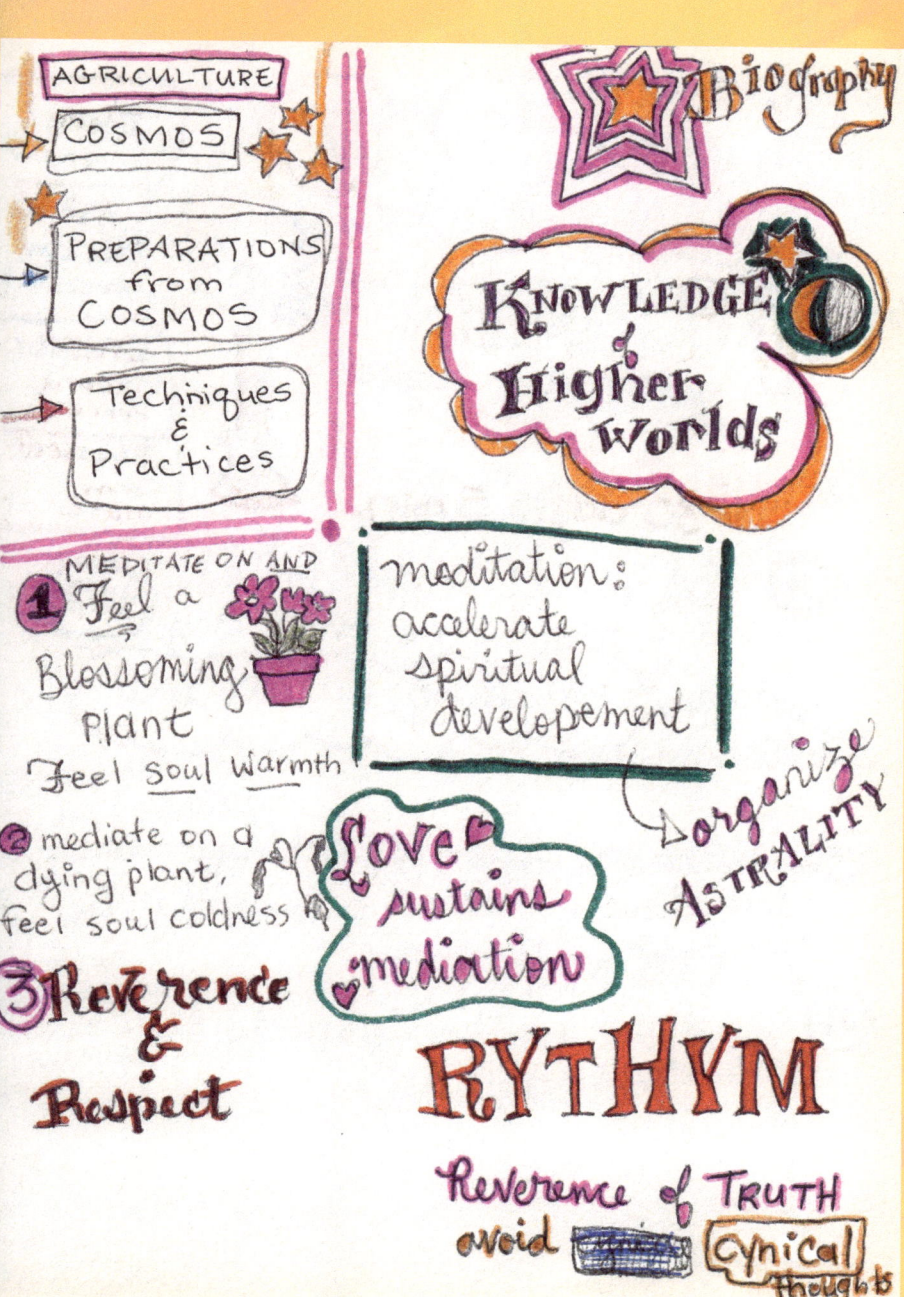

AGRICULTURE

COSMOS

PREPARATIONS
from
COSMOS

Techniques
&
Practices

Biography

KNOWLEDGE
of
Higher
worlds

MEDITATE ON AND

① Feel a
Blossoming
Plant
Feel soul warmth

meditation:
accelerate
spiritual
developement

Jorganize
ASTRALITY

② mediate on a
dying plant,
feel soul coldness

Love
sustains
mediation

③ Reverence
&
Respect

RYTHM

Reverence of TRUTH
avoid Cynical
thoughts

LOGICAL THINKING

will in our thinking

① Pick an object and describe it in an organized, logical fashion.

30 days, 5 min.

I-level inventor

Astral design necessity

ETHERIC History Process

Physical form, material

② Pick an action to do at the same time every day.

Will

Perserverance *thinking in our will*

③ master expression of feelings, so that those expressed outwardly are those you determine

④ Find the positive aspects of everything.

Try one day, one week
dedicated or
to each Even
ONE
↳ MONTH

SIX·FOLD·PATH

Chakra
OF
THE
HEART

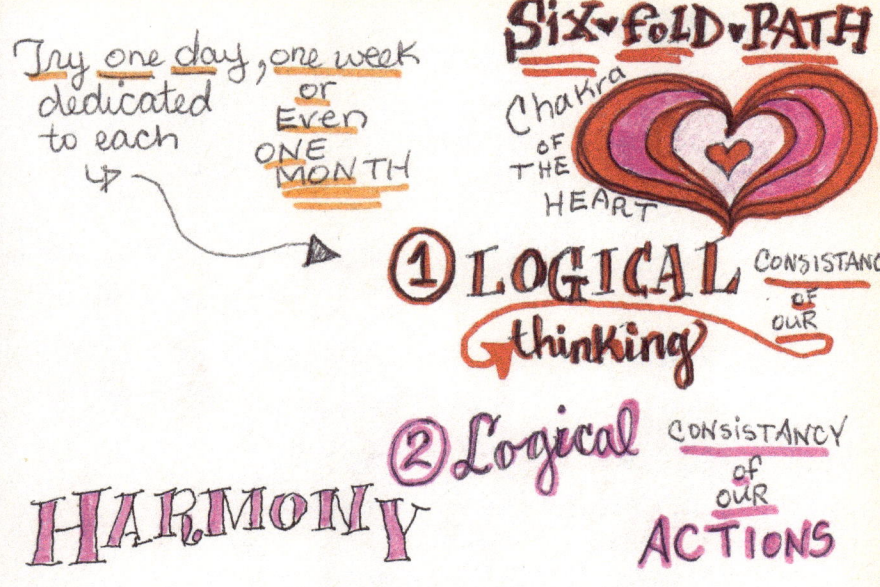

① LOGICAL CONSISTANCY
OF
OUR

thinking

② *Logical* CONSISTANCY
OF
OUR
ACTIONS

HARMONY

③ QUALITY of OUR
PERSERVERANCE

Perserverance
is the capacity
to sustain a
course of action
despite failure
provided I
continue to
believe it is
the right task

④ OPEN mindedness

⑤ POSITIVITY

⑥ Tranquility

wisdom
lives
in
flowing
Light

Enliven GEOGRAPHY

GEOGRAPHY

GRAPHIC LESSONS

VEGETATION

PRODUCTS

① Describe country
② Draw
③ Have children draw map on board
④ TRAVEL BOOKS!
  ↳ create travel brochures
   Country presentations
   Where have I been?
   where would I like to go.

8 FOLD PATH COME FROM BUDDHA

① Truth value of thoughts
② Care resolves
③ Humanity + Percision of ➤ SPEECH
④ Balance inner + outer culture
⑤ management of all of Life
⑥ Leading Edge → CHALLENGE
⑦ Learner *CONSTANTLY LEARN*
⑧ Inner Audit (once a month) what do I want?
  KNOWLEDGE? strengths?

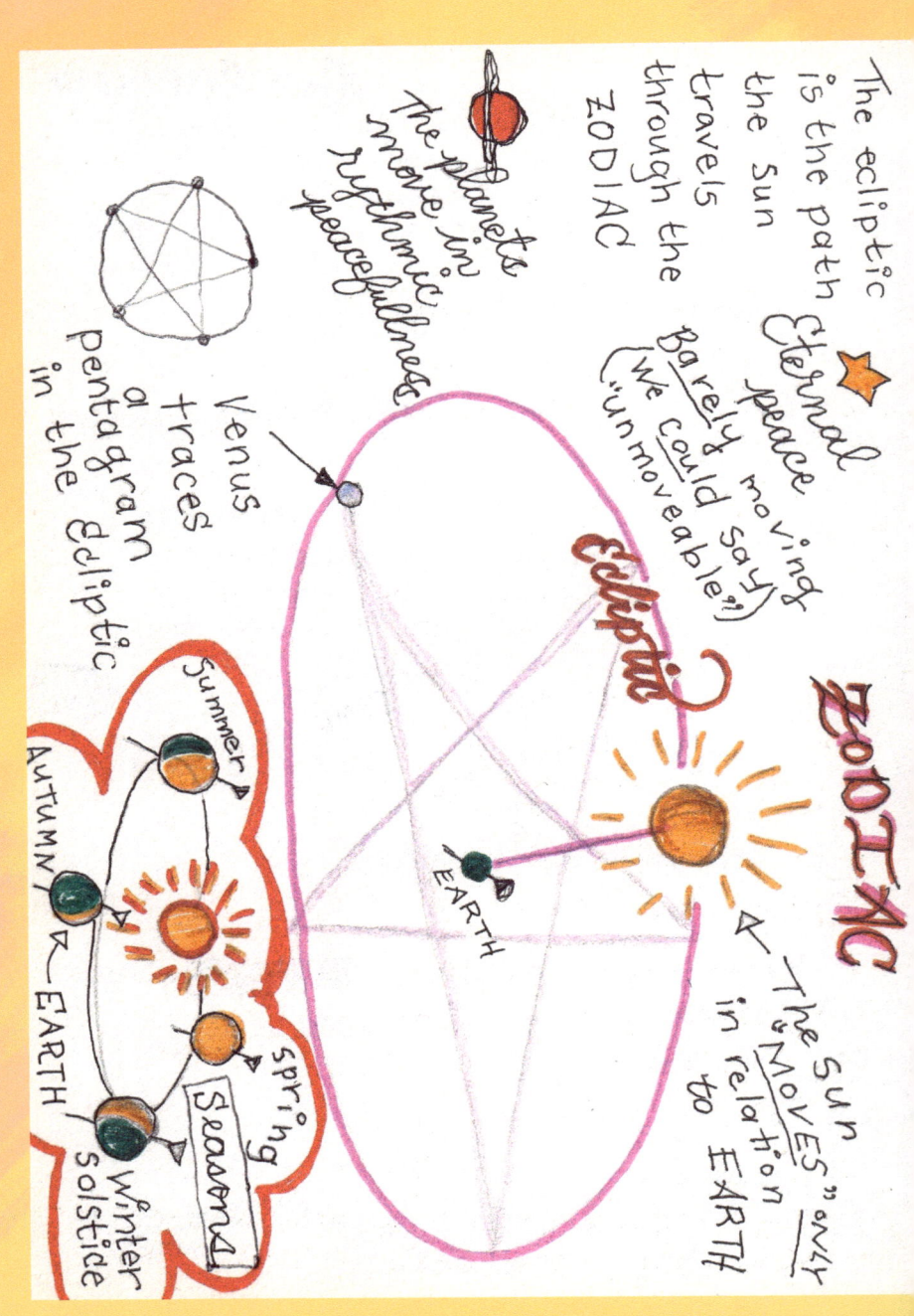

The ecliptic is the path the Sun travels through the ZODIAC

Eternal peace
Barely moving
(we could say)
("unmoveable")

The planets move in rythmic peacefullness

Venus traces a pentagram in the ecliptic

ZODIAC

Ecliptic

EARTH

← The Sun "MOVES" only in relation to EARTH

Summer

AUTUMN ← EARTH

Spring

Seasons

Winter solstice

FABLES & STORIES

Introduce stories & Fables

DON'T explain.

Fables can end with a picture as they are so short.

If you climbed into the pen with a bull, what would happen?

FABLES
1. Tell fable and Draw Picture
2. WRITE paragraph
3. Questions

* NATURALIST BOOKS FROM VICTORIAN TIMES

OAK

aquatic grass

Reeds

The Oak and the reeds.

→ Compare to humans

TALL Strong

← Bend

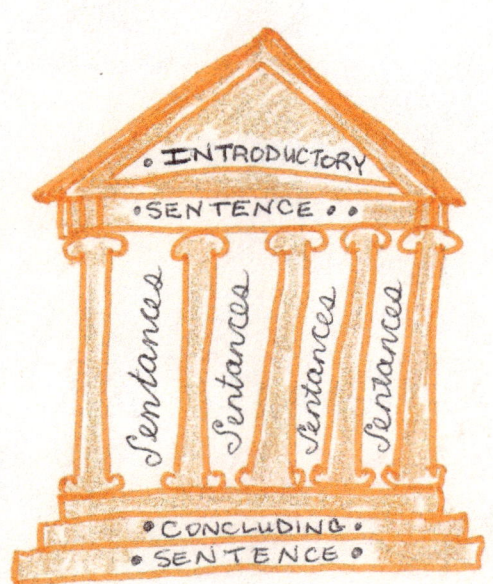

In ancient Greece people built temples to be so beautiful that the Gods' could not ▓▓ resist entering. So we CONSTRUCT ~~▓▓▓▓▓~~ our paragraphs to be beautiful, inviting the divine, and others, into understanding what we write.

★ Oh be joyful oh be jubilant
★ Put your sorrows far away
★ Come rejoice and sing
   together
★ On this day

Festivals ★

- anticipation
- reverence
- wonder

oedipus Rex by ARISTOTL } The Problem

OPPOSITES

DESIRE ⟩ LOVE ⟨ HATE

FEAR ⟩ COURAGE ⟨ RECKLESS

LAUGHTER elation ⟩ Saelde ⟨ WEEPING depression

Blessedness

SHAME ⟩   ⟨ Indifference

                 ⟨ Contra-social

Social ⟩

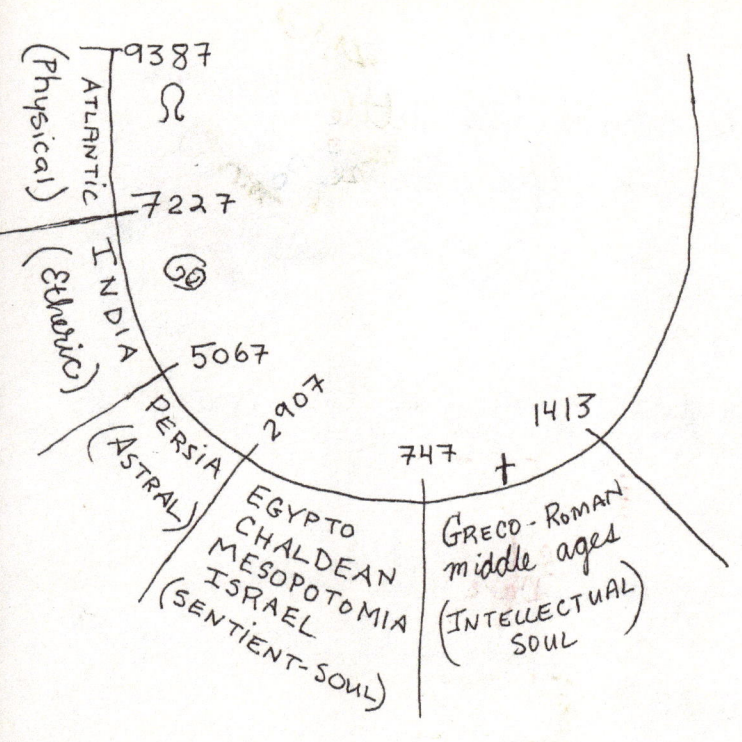

ATLANTIC (Physical)

9387

♌

7227

INDIA (Etheric)

♋

5067

PERSIA (ASTRAL)

2907

EGYPTO
CHALDEAN
MESOPOTOMIA
ISRAEL
(SENTIENT-SOUL)

747

✝

1413

GRECO - ROMAN
middle ages
(INTELLECTUAL)
SOUL

Let's make our little
Thank you House

1, 2, 3
Thank you for the meal

1 2 3
gražias por la comida

1, 2, 3
merci pour le bon repas

Don't
use
Point
"Baby Bear"

Work from Body

"WHOLE"
not outlines

VEGETARIAN

A good Choice! With Balance

makes our Etheric work Harder!

(modern day) with problems such as pesticides, fertilizers etc, are vegetables even capable of sustaining life?

less damaging to eat meat than abstain for righteous reasons.

"vegetarianism is best for those engaged in intellectual OR spiritual work"

Breakfast
—no sugar,
no eggs,
oatmeal
vegetables

An individuals own inner spiritual activity takes part in directing the satisfaction of his own nutritional needs.

"Presence"
by
OTTO Scharmer

For the Golden corn
and the apples on the tree
For the yellow butter
and the honey for my tea
For fruits and nuts and berries
that grow along the way
For birds and bees and
Flowers
We give thanks
Every day.

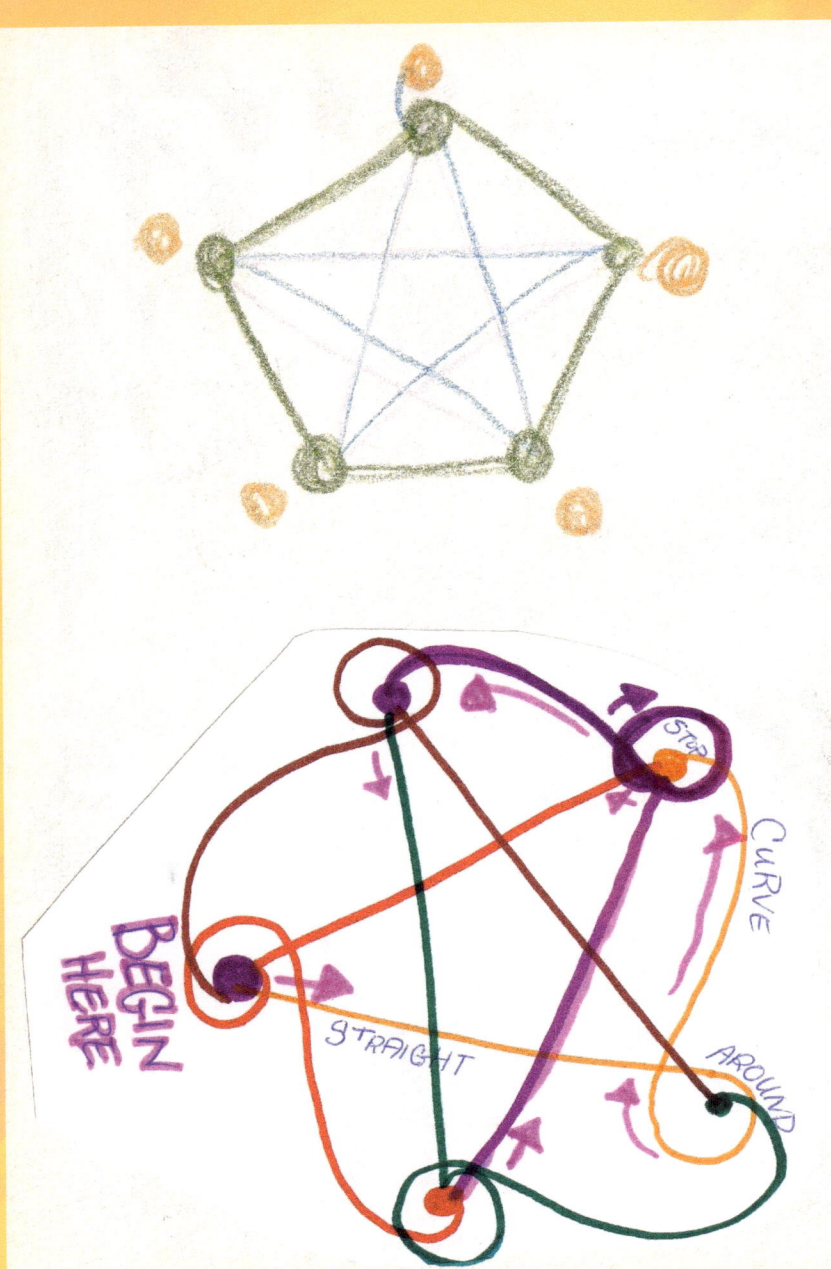

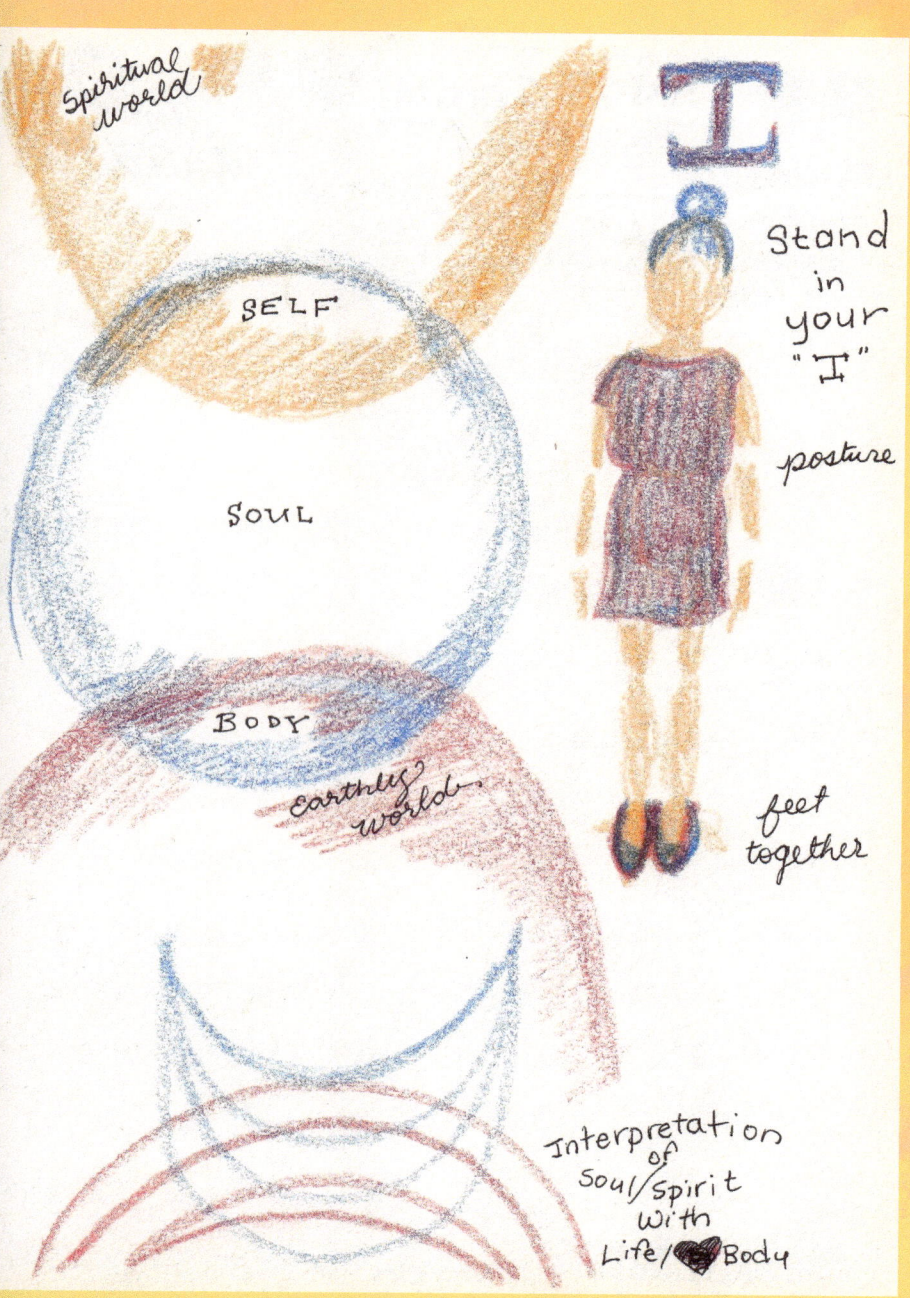

Spiritual world

SELF

SOUL

BODY

earthly world

Stand
in
your
"I"

posture

feet
together

Interpretation
of
Soul/Spirit
with
Life/♥ Body

Rückshau!

Frees
the
Etheric

BACK WARDS ⬆

LOOK ⬆

an
Antidote

Distraction Dragon

18 Breaths
Per minute

1080 Breaths
Per HOUR

25,960
BREATHS
per
Day.

We are
embedded
in the
COSMOS

PRECESSION of the Equinoxs
⊕ ✷ PLATONIC YEAR ◯ 🪐 ✷

25,000 years
one cycle of the equinox
around the ecliptic

25,920 a
Number
of
Breaths
per
Day.

The GREAT

A traditional name for WHEN the
planets and fixed stars
complete a cycle and return
to a configuration they have
held before.

∘ ONE ∘ COSMIC ∘ DAY ∘   ONE WORLD. WE
ARE ALL CONNECTED.

INCARNATION

MAYA: a protective environment

Animals

ANCIENT EARTH

Plant stage

Ancient Moon

Ancient Sun

Ancient Saturn

Physical Universe "A GIFT"

Etheric Body Begins "A GIFT"

S

S

M

E

Love Conciousness

ASTRAL SPIRIT "A GIFT" MIND

"I AM" ETERNAL EGO

Ego-creation

COSMOS

SPIRIT-SELF

FREE BEINGS: HUMANS

TO BE SEPARATE

Put your EGO IN SERVICE.
What is our way to serve?
... FORMING A BEING NEEDS TO BE SEPARATE

polarity

At the
moment
of
BIRTH...
Perfection

Soul
Spirit
Kernal (germ)

DEVOTION

STRIVING

LOVE
HEART
WILL

Acceptance

physical
GROWTH
DEVELOPMENT
FUTURE

consciousness
WISDOM

names
FROM PAST

Give
Surrender

MORAL
consciousness

Give thanks to
Mother Earth
Give thanks to
Father Sun
Give thanks to
the flowers in the Garden
Where the Mother
and the Father are one.

RESOURCES ★★★

waldorflibrary.org

JAN STUDET

r steiner archives.org

VICTOR BORGE: GRAMMAR PUNCUATION

Allan Howard "Nativity"

AWSNA — Getting! to yes!

HARRAR

"See how they move." by Magda Gerber

"Free self-initiated movement" safe, free play

KOVACS

Steiner Waldorf curriculum: RAWSON & Richter

"Games children play"

"And then take hands" Molly H.

Sylvia Ashton Warner teacher

The Art of LIVING

"Blue Book of Waldorf Curriculum"

Difficult conversations

"Sing me the creation" PAUL MATTHEW

The therapeutic eye.

★Peter Selg

Kristoff Jaffke

Developing the observing eye cynthia murphy Lang

Constructing the universe

Journalist writing about Waldorf matt Richtel

Taylor Mali Poems on teaching

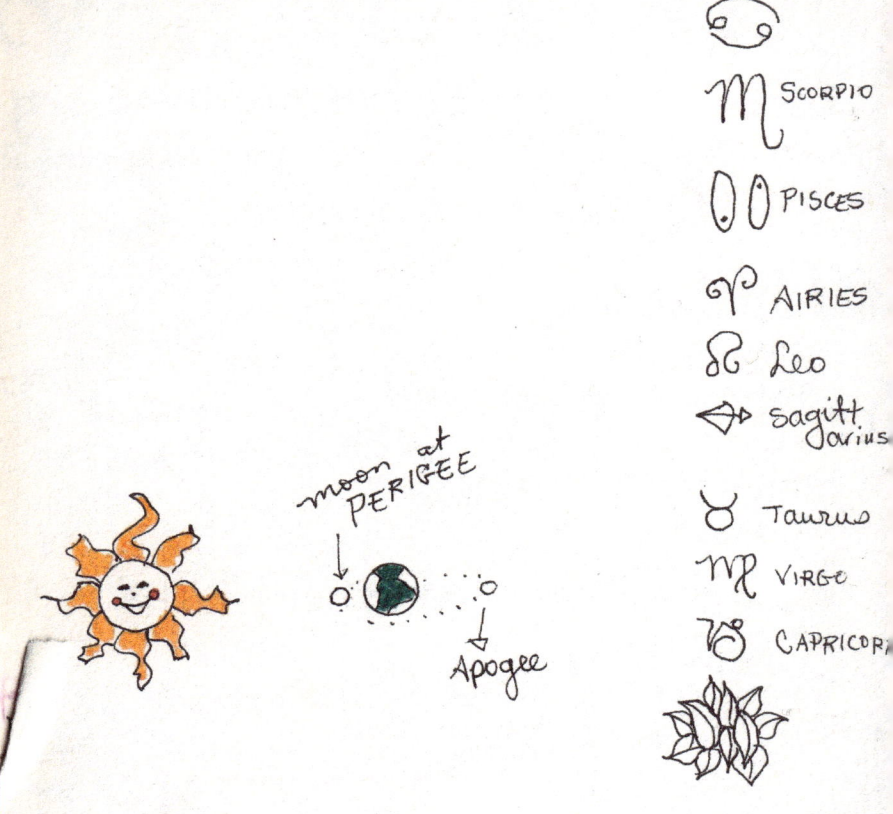

CANCER

SCORPIO

PISCES

AIRIES

Leo

sagitt arius

Taurus

VIRGO

CAPRICORN

Verse given by Rudolf Steiner: for Laura Lavender.

"We must eradicate from the soul all fear and terror of what comes towards us out of the future. We must aquire serenity in all feelings and sensations about the future. We must look forward with absolute equanimity to all that may come, and we must think only that whatever comes is given to us by a world direction full of wisdom.

It is part of what we must learn in this age, namely, to live out of pure trust without any security in material existance, trusting the ever-present help of the spiritual world. Truly, nothing else will do if our courage is not to fail us. Let us discipline our will, and let us seek the awakening from within, every morning and every evening."

✦☽ ZODIAC ☾✦

PISCES fishes	♓	water, leaf ♦ (DAMP)
ARIES Ram	♈	warm, fruit ☌ (HOT)
TAURUS Bull	♉	Earth Root ⚷ (COLD)
GEMINI twins	♊	Light Flower ⚘ (AIR)
CANCER crab	♋	water, leaf ♦
LEO Lion	♌	warm, fruit ☌
VIRGO virgin	♍	Earth, root ⚷
LIBRA Scales	♎	Light, flower ⚘

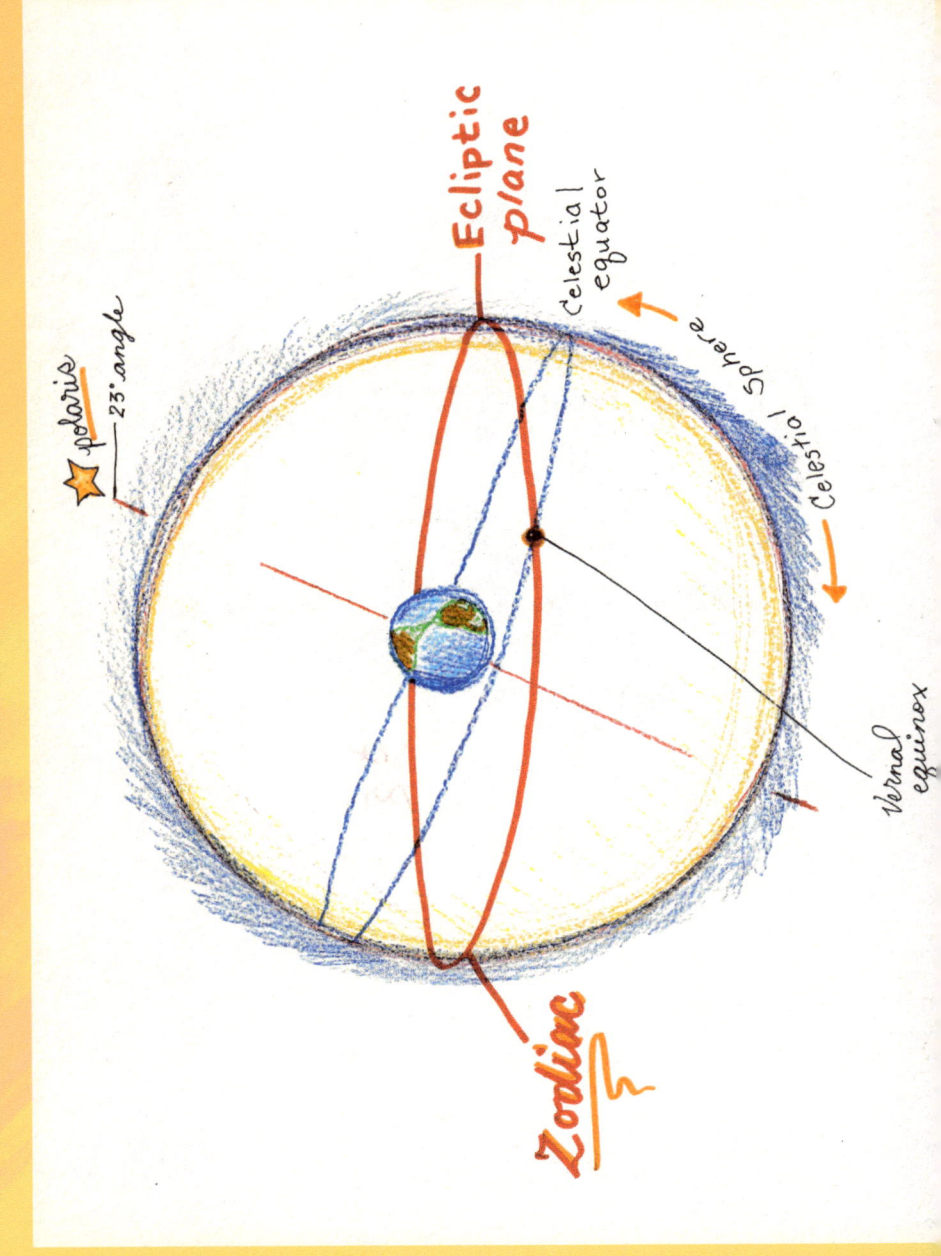

SCORPIO ♏︎   water, leaf ♏
Scorpion

SAGITTARIUS ♐   warm, fruit ♉
archer

CAPRICORN ♑   Earth, root ♈
goat

AQUARIUS ♒   Light, flower ✿
waterman

EARTH Root	LIGHT Flower	WATER leaf
♉ taurus	♊ gemini	♋ crab
♑ capricorn	♎ libra	♓ pisces
♍ virgo	♒ aquarius	♏ scorpio
Bees: COMB	Bees: pollen	Bees: HONEY

WARM fruit
♌ Leo
♈ Aries
♐ Archer

Bees:
fruit = nectar

☿ MERCURY

♀ VENUS

⊕ EARTH

♂ MARS

♃ Jupiter

♄ Saturn

♅ URANUS

♆ Neptune

♇ pluto

Laura is a calligrapher and illustrator
living in a colourful Victorian house in
Nova Scotia, Canada. A lifelong artistic
soul, the first art project she remembers
creating as a child was a portrait of
her mother, with a pregnant belly that
folded open to reveal the unborn baby
brother within. She is also an avid organic
beekeeper, and certified Waldorf teacher,
a long-term goal fulfilled!